500
Genetics
Questions

Jeffry L. Shultz, Ph.D.

Other Titles by Dr. Shultz Available on Amazon

X-Linked, Y-Linked and Mitochondrial Inheritance Pedigree Workbook

Autosomal Recessive Pedigree Workbook

SSR and SNP Molecular Marker Pedigree Workbook

300 Blank Pedigrees

Genetics: Core Concepts (Kindle Format)

Cover art: The merging galaxy system Arp 220 from ALMA and Hubble.jpg
Hubble: Public Domain via Wikimedia Commons.
ALMA Observatory. Public domain, via Wikimedia Commons CC 4.0;
https://commons.wikimedia.org/wiki/File:The_merging_galaxy_system_Arp_220_from_ALMA_and_
Hubble.jpg

Table of Contents

Using This Book

Disclaimer

This book was created as a supplemental learning/assessment resource: I have created **OTHER** versions of each question; **ONE** is exclusive to this book; **ONE** is available as a *study* question in a Genetics course available from TopHat (created by myself) and **MORE** are used as variants in the associated TopHat exams. What does this mean? It means that the questions in this book are available to *anyone*; If you use this material for an exam, you must assume that within a short time the students at your institution will be aware of this book and *will have an answer key to your exam*.....:-o

Educators

The questions in this book are organized by subject, then by type. The pages are formatted so that you can copy a single page and combine single pages into a test. Each question has a unique code; the answers are organized based on these codes, allowing you to more easily create a key for your exam.

Students

Use the table of contents to identify where the questions are located that you wish to study. Be aware that there are *substantial* differences in difficulty in the questions; Try a page of questions, then check the answers to make sure that you are on the right track.

Foils

In order to discover how thorough your knowledge of a subject is, sometimes a term or group of terms that *sounds* like it should be something is used; for instance, "ribosomal polymerase reaction" sounds like it is *something*, but it is simply a combination of terms that do not mean *anything*. It combines "ribosomal" and parts of the "polymerase chain reaction (PCR)" into a combined word salad that is *meaningless*......

Near Duplicates

You may notice that several questions are similar to each other. Although we hope for the best from our students, the temptation of close proximity during an exam can lead to students looking at other students' answers. The same question with "heterozygous" can be changed to "homozygous" or "hemizygous" and completely change the answer. This increases the difficulty of cheating, because now students must read the other *question* as well. This technique also works for timed, digitally administered exams.

Central Dogma True/False (CTF)

CTF1 ___ The following sequences are possible (True) or not possible (False)
5' - UCGAUCAG - 3' mRNA
3' - TCGATCAG - 5' coding DNA
5' - AGCTAGTC - 3' template DNA

CTF2 ___ The following sequences are possible (True) or not possible (False)
5' - ACGACGAAG - 3' mRNA
5' - ACGACGAAG - 3' coding DNA
3' - TGCTGCTTC - 5' template DNA

CTF3 ___ The following sequences are possible (True) or not possible (False)
5' - UCGUCGUUG - 3' mRNA
5' - ACGACGAAG - 3' coding DNA
3' - TGCTGCTTC - 5' template DNA

CTF4 ___ The following sequences are possible (True) or not possible (False)
5' - M I R... -3 polypeptide (partial)
5' - AUGAUCCGU - 3' mRNA
5' - ATGATCCGT - 3' coding DNA
3' - TACTAGGCA - 5' template DNA

CTF5 ___ The following sequences are possible (True) or not possible (False)
5' - UCGAUCAG - 3' mRNA
5' - TCGATCAG - 3' coding DNA
3' - AGCTAGTC - 5' template DNA

CTF6 ___ The following sequences are possible (True) or not possible (False)
5' - M T R... -3 polypeptide (partial)
5' - AUGACCUGU - 3' mRNA
5' - ATGACCTGT - 3' coding DNA
3' - TACTGGACA - 5' template DNA

CTF7 ___ The following sequences are possible (True) or not possible (False)
5' - UCGATCAG - 3' mRNA
5' - TCGATCAG - 3' coding DNA
3' - AGCTAGTC - 5' template DNA

CTF8 ___ The following sequences are possible (True) or not possible (False)
5' - GAAGCAGCA - 3' mRNA
5' - GAAGCAGCA - 3' coding DNA
3' - TGCTGCTTC - 5' template DNA

CTF9 ___ In DNA gel electrophoresis, samples run towards negative/red (True/False)

CTF10 ___ Griffith discovered that the transforming material was RNA (True/False)

CTF11 ___ Watson and Crick discovered that DNA was replicated in a conservative manner (True/False)

CTF12 ___ Avery, Macleod and McCarty discovered that DNA was responsible for Griffiths transformation experiment (True/False)

CTF13 ___ Prokaryote RNA has multiple origins of replication (True/False)

CTF14 ___ Prokaryote DNA is linear in form (True/False)

CTF15 ___ Eukaryote DNA has multiple origins of replication (True/False)

CTF16 ___ Housekeeping genes are always expressed (True/False)

CTF17 ___ Housekeeping genes are differentially expressed (True/False)

CTF18 ___ Alternative splicing means an intron can be left in edited rRNA (True/False)

CTF19 ___ Alternative splicing means that an exon can be removed from a transcript (True/False)

CTF20 ___ RNA polymerase III is required for mRNA synthesis (True/False)

CTF21 ___ RNA polymerase II is required for tRNA synthesis (True/False)

CTF22 ___ A heated lid on a PCR machine is used to keep your samples from evaporating (True/False)

CTF23 ___ The RNA induced silencing complex (RISC) is used with microRNA to regulate mRNA (True/False)

CTF24 ___ There are several exceptions to the codons used for polypeptide synthesis (True/False)

CTF25 ___ A charged mRNA brings an amino acid in to a ribosome for incorporation into a polypeptide (True/False)

CTF26 ___ Non-disjunction during meiosis I results in 0% viable gametes (True/False)

CTF27 ___ Non-disjunction during meiosis II results in 0% viable gametes (True/False)

CTF28 ___ An acrocentric eukaryote chromosome has a centromere and a telomere (True/False)

CTF29 ___ A eukaryote chromosome has a centromere and 2 telomeres (True/False)

CTF30 ___ A euploid Human female karyotype has 47 chromosomes (True/False)

Central Dogma Multiple Choice (CM)

CM1 ___ The process that utilizes DNA polymerase is:
A   mitosis   D   meiosis II
B   transcription   E   All of the above
C   Ribosomal Polymerase Reaction

CM2 ___ Molecule(s) required for meiosis I and mitosis:
A   DNA polymerase   D   tRNA
B   RNA polymerase   E   mRNA
C   Ribosomes

CM3 ___ You need this molecule to make microRNA
A   DNA polymerase   D   tRNA
B   DNA Template   E   mRNA
C   Ribosomes

CM4 ___ This molecule is NOT required to make a polypeptide
A   rRNA   D   mRNA
B   tRNA   E   All are required to make a polypeptide
C   DNA Polymerase

CM5 ___ RNA polymerase is not required for which of the following
A   mRNA   D   RNAse
B   tRNA   E   rRNA
C   microRNA

CM6 ___ The process regulated by microRNA is:
A   translation   D   meiosis I
B   transcription   E   All of the above
C   transpiration

CM7 ___ The process associated with ribosomes is:
A   mitosis   D   Meiosis II
B   transcription   E   All of the above
C   translation

CM8 ___ The process associated with RNA polymerase is:
A   mitosis   D   meiosis II
B   transcription   E   All of the above
C   translation

CM9 ___ The process interrupted by siRNA is:
A   DNA Replication   D   meiosis II
B   transcription   E   All of the above
C   translation

CM10 ___ Which of the following is needed to perform PCR (may be more than one)?
A   Ribosome   D   Primers
B   DNA polymerase   E   Topoisomerase
C   RNA polymerase I

CM11 ___ Which process does not require complementary base pairing?
A   DNA Replication   D   topoisomerase
B   siRNA regulation   E   All require complementary base pairing
C   transcription

CM12 ___ Commonly used name for a PCR machine
A   DNA Doubler   D   Thermal Cycler
B   Mullis-Microwave   E   None of the above
C   Taq cycler

CM13 ___ What could cause all transcription to stop in a prokaryote?
A   The sole RNA polymerase gene has mutated
B   siRNA production has stopped
C   A promoter sequence in front of the sole Gln-tRNA encoding gene has mutated
D   A specific transcription factor is missing
E   All of the above

CM14 ___ You have detected a 10-fold decrease in siRNA production in human cancer cells vs a control. What could this mean?
A   Overall RNA production has increased in the cancer subject
B   A specific cellular reproduction gene is no longer being regulated
C   A group of cellular control genes are being silenced
D   The cellular mechanisms controlling tRNA production may have been damaged
E   DNA polymerase is being controlled by the siRNA

CM15 ___ You have performed an extraction of a eukaryote cells' RNA - you discover that there are no mRNA molecules - what is the most likely cause of this?
A   All of the tRNA genes have become mutated
B   All of the mRNA genes have become mutated
C   The RNA polymerase I genes have been inactivated
D   The RNA polymerase II genes have been inactivated
E   The RNA polymerase III genes have been inactivated

CM16 ___ You have performed a test on a patient and found that the mRNA of a suspect gene in a pathway has a normal transcription level; Which of the following could be the cause of the disease if it is in fact caused by this gene?
A   siRNA is reducing suspect gene polypeptide production
B   microRNA is reducing suspect gene polypeptide production
C   The suspect gene mRNA encodes a defective poplypeptide
D   Either A or B
E   All of the above

CM17 ___ Incorporation of amino acids into a growing polypeptide has stopped, which one of the following molecules is most likely lacking in the cell?
A   microRNA   D   charged tRNA
B   ribosome   E   rRNA
C   polysome

CM18 ____ You notice a missing chromosome in a patients karyotype - which of these conditions is caused by monosomy?

A   Patau Syndrome   D   Parkinsons Disease
B   Turner Syndrome   E   All of the above are possible
C   Huntingtons Disease

CM19 ____ Which of the following represents the best possible (not likely to be random) "e" value from a BLAST result?

A   0.15   D   7e-150
B   6.1   E   6e-24
C   0.0

CM20 ____ Which of these Hardy-Weinberg assumptions has changed the most in Humans over the past 300 years?

A   Mitigation   D   Mutation
B   Artificial Selection   E   All have changed extensively
C   Migration

CM21 ____ You wish to study a previously undiscovered organism. Which data would give you a quick overview of what the organism transcribes to compare with other, known organisms?

A   rRNA sequencing   D   Sanger DNA genomic sequencing
B   tRNA sequencing   E   All of the above
C   EST sequencing

CM22 ____ The temperature required to separate two complementary strands of the same DNA molecule is affected by which of the following factors?

A   The direction of the strand   D   The availability of DNA helicase
B   The A/C content of the strand   E   The availability of DNA Polymerase
C   The A/T content of the strand

CM23 ____ You have read a report that indicates your genome of interest has a 60% G/C content. What is the percent of the genome that is Guanine?

A   60%   D   30%
B   20%   E   40%
C   35%

CM24 ____ In a diploid cell, mitosis leads to:

A   Four haploid gametes   D   Four daughter cells
B   Two daughter cells   E   Two haploid gametes
C   One diploid daughter cell and two haploid gametes

CM25 ____ In the scientific method, once you have identified a problem, what is the next step?

A   Perform the experiment, collecting data
B   Reformulate hypothesis; re-test as necessary
C   Propose a testable hypothesis (solution)
D   Design a controlled experiment
E   Interpret the data, compare to expected results

CM26 ____ Cancer is caused by uncontrolled cell growth, which core concept of Genetics is vital to understanding what causes this condition?

A   Polymerase chain reaction   D   Mendelian Genetics
B   Transmission Genetics   E   none of the above
C   The Hardy-Weinberg Equilibrium

The genetic code (standard codon table):

First				
U	UUU, UUC — Phenylalanine (F, Phe) (4.0%); UUA, UUG, CUU, CUC, CUA, CUG — Leucine (L, Leu) (9.3%)	UCU, UCC, UCA, UCG — Serine (S, Ser) (7.0%)	UAU, UAC — Tyrosine (Y, Tyr) (3.0%); UAA, UAG — STOP	UGU, UGC — Cysteine (C, Cys) (1.9%); UGA — STOP; UGG — Tryptophan (W, Trp) (1.3%)
C	CUU, CUC, CUA, CUG — Leucine (L, Leu) (9.3%)	CCU, CCC, CCA, CCG — Proline (P, Pro) (5.1%)	CAU, CAC — Histidine (H, His) (7.8%); CAA, CAG — Glutamine (Q, Gln) (3.7%)	CGU, CGC, CGA, CGG — Arginine (R, Arg) (5.3%)
A (START)	AUU, AUC, AUA — Isoleucine (I, Ile) (5.7%); AUG — Methionine (M, Met) (2.4%)	ACU, ACC, ACA, ACG — Threonine (T, Thr) (5.5%)	AAU, AAC — Asparagine (N, Asn) (4.5%); AAA, AAG — Lysine (K, Lys) (5.4%)	AGA, AGG — Arginine (R, Arg) (5.3%); AGU, AGC — Serine (S, Ser) (7.0%)
G	GUU, GUC, GUA, GUG — Valine (V, Val) (6.2%)	GCU, GCC, GCA, GCG — Alanine (A, Ala) (8.6%)	GAU, GAC — Aspartic Acid (D, Asp) (5.0%); GAA, GAG — Glutamic Acid (E, Glu) (6.1%)	GGU, GGC, GGA, GGG — Glycine (G, Gly) (6.7%)

Non-Polar   Polar   Aromatic   Basic   Acidic

© J. L. Shultz

CM27 ____ Given the following DNA coding sequence **5' - CGATGATTCCTCATTGT - 3'**, what is the resulting polypeptide in single letter annotation (beginning from the start codon only)?

- A   5'-MFLIV -3'
- B   5'-MIPHC...-3'
- C   5'-GCTACTAAGGAGTAACA-3'
- D   5'-ACAATGAGGAATCATCG -3'
- E   None of the above

CM28 ____ Given the following DNA coding sequence **5' - CGATGTTCCTCATTGTC - 3'**, what is the resulting polypeptide in single letter annotation (beginning from the start codon only)?

- A   5'-MFLIV -3'
- B   5'-MIPHC...-3'
- C   5'-GCTACTAAGGAGTAACA-3'
- D   5'-ACAATGAGGAATCATCG -3'
- E   None of the above

CM29 ____ The following is an mRNA sequence. What was the CODING sequence?

5'- AUGGAAAACGUUGA - 3'

- A   5'- ATGGAAAACGTTGA - 3'
- B   5'- TACCTTTTGCAACT - 3'
- C   3'- TACCTTTTGCAACT - 5'
- D   5'- AGTTGCAAAAGGTA - 3'
- E   The sequence is not listed in A-D

CM30 ____ Which of the following are required for a population to be in genetic equilibrium (More than one may be selected)?

- A   No Mutation
- B   Survival of the fastest
- C   No Natural Selection
- D   Mitigation
- E   Sufficient Population size (aka no genetic drift)
- F   Random Mating
- G   Artificial Selection
- H   No Migration

BMC Cancer 2015, 15:597

Comparison of the prognosis and recurrence of apparent early-stage ovarian tumors treated with laparoscopy and laparotomy: a meta-analysis of clinical studies

Ying Zhang, Shuying Fan, Yang Xiang, Hua Duan and Li Sun

Background

This meta-analysis aimed to evaluate the prognosis and recurrence of apparent early-stage ovarian tumors treated with laparoscopy compared with laparotomy.

Methods

Clinical studies published in English were retrieved from the computerized databases Medline and Embase. A meta-analysis was performed to investigate the differences in the efficacy and safety of laparoscopy versus laparotomy in terms of postoperative complications, lengths of hospital stay, recurrence rates, and disease-free survival times using the random effects model. The studies were independently reviewed by two investigators. Data from the eligible studies were extracted, and the meta-analysis was performed using the Comprehensive Meta-Analysis program, version 2 (CMA-2; Biostat, Englewood, NJ, USA).

Results

A total of 8 studies were included in the analysis. The results showed that laparoscopic surgery was significantly associated with lower rates of complications (OR = 0.433, P = 0.019) and shorter postoperative hospital stays (weighted mean difference [WMD] = −0.974, P < 0.001). There was no significant difference in the rates of recurrence (OR = 0.707, P = 0.521) between patients with apparent early-stage ovarian tumors who were treated using laparoscopy and those who underwent laparotomy. No publication bias was detected.

Conclusions

Laparoscopic surgery shows favorable prognostic outcomes in terms of postoperative complication rates and postoperative hospital stay durations. Further studies with longer follow-up periods are required to confirm recurrence and survival outcomes after laparoscopic surgery in patients with apparent early-stage ovarian tumors.

CM31 ___ What would SUPPORT the findings of Zhang et als.' BMC paper above?

A   Discovering that the authors perform only laparoscopy surgeries

B   Discovering that the project was paid for by a company that supplies laparoscopic surgery kits

C   A second paper that uses the third version of the CMA program (CMA-3) showing the same general trend

D   Finding out that the authors are not from America

E   None of the above

CM32 ___ Which of the following is more closely related to mRNA?

A   ribosomal RNA   D   Amino Acids
B   complementary DNA   E   all of the above
C   consensus DNA

CM33 ___ You are studying a new organism. You notice that there are more unique polypeptides than genes - what could be the reason for this?

A   Codon Bias   D   Alternative splicing
B   microRNA   E   All of the above
C   siRNA

CM34 ___ Which of the following represent applied research?
   A   Describing the structure of kinetochores
   B   Identifying the molecules involved in transcription
   C   Finding the gene responsible for cystic fibrosis
   D   Identifying the molecules involved in translation
   E   None of the above

CM35 ___ Which of the following represent basic research (More than one may be selected)?
   A   Describing the structure of kinetochores
   B   Identifying the molecules involved in transcription
   C   Finding the gene responsible for cystic fibrosis
   D   Identifying the molecules involved in translation
   E   None of the above

CM36 ___ Which of the following represents Peer Review?
   A   Discussing the outcome of an experiment with another student
   B   Noticing that the lab protocol has an error
   C   Reading a manuscript for a class discussion
   D   Reading a manuscript for inclusion in a report
   E   All of the above

CM37 ___ After reading a manuscript, you realize that they used the wrong Human population in their study. This is an example of:
   A   Basic Research   D   An interpretation of the results
   B   Peer review   E   All of the above
   C   Poor data collection

CM38 ___ You have identified a disease that you want to investigate (and maybe cure!). Which of the following is a testable applied research hypothesis?
   A   Identify who has the disease
   B   Find a gene that underlies the phenotype
   C   Find out where humans with the disease are geographically located
   D   Identify the enzymatic pathway that causes the phenotype
   E   All of the above

CM39 ___ A mutation is important for which of the following fields of Genetics?
   A   Transmission Genetics   D   A-C are all mutation-based
   B   Population Genetics   E   None of the above are affected by mutation
   C   The Central Dogma

CM40 ___ You read a study that compares two surgical procedures and their respective outcomes. Their data is derived from English-language journals. What effect does the fact that English-language only journals were used have on this study? (Multiple answers possible)
   A   It renders the results applicable to English-only regions
   B   It has no bearing on the conclusions of this paper
   C   It opens up the possibility of performing the same type of research using non-English sources.
   D   It means that environmental factors such as nutrition, medical care, environmental quality) may be different and could affect the results if non-English journals are used.
   E   All of the above

CM41 ____ Discovered that DNA was the genetic material
A   Franklin   D   Watson and Crick
B   Griffith   E   Chargaff
C   Avery, MaCleod, McCarty

CM42 ____ Discovered that DNA had equal amounts of Adenine and Thymine
A   Mendel   D   Meselson and Stahl
B   Griffith   E   Chargaff
C   Avery, MaCleod, McCarty

CM43 ____ Identified segregation patterns in pea plants
A   Mendel   D   Watson and Crick
B   Griffith   E   Chargaff
C   Avery, MaCleod, McCarty

CM44 ____ Discovered the structure of DNA
A   Mendel   D   Watson and Crick
B   Griffith   E   Chargaff
C   Avery, MaCleod, McCarty

CM45 ____ Discovered the helical form of DNA
A   Mendel   D   Franklin
B   Griffith   E   Chargaff
C   Avery, MaCleod, McCarty

CM46 ____ Which of the following carry out their functions in the cytoplasm?
A   microRNA   D   mRNA
B   siRNA   E   All carry out their functions in the cytoplasm
C   tRNA

CM47 ____ Which of the following are created in the nucleus?
A   microRNA   D   mRNA
B   rRNA   E   All are created in the nucleus
C   tRNA

CM48 ____ Which of the following are not exported from the nucleus?
A   microRNA   D   mRNA
B   Introns   E   All are exported from the nucleus
C   Exons

CM49 ____ You have a gene with 15 exons. How many introns are in this gene?
A   5   D   16
B   3   E   Unable to determine
C   14

CM50 ____ You have a gene with 15 introns. How many exons are in this gene?
A   5   D   16
B   3   E   Unable to determine
C   14

CM51 ____ What percentage of mice survived the Avery et al. experiments?
A   0%   D   75%
B   25%   E   100%
C   50%

CM52 ___ What percentage of mice survived the Griffith experiments?

A 0% D 75%

B 25% E 100%

C 50%

CM53 ___ In the Avery et al. experiments, removal of which molecule from the heat-killed mixture led to the isolation of type IIIS bacteria from dead mice?

A Polysaccharides D All of the above

B Protein E None of the above

C RNA

CM54 ___ In the Griffith experiment, which treatment led to isolation of type IIIS bacteria from dead mice?

A Infection with type IIIR bacteria

B Combined Infection with living type IIIS bacteria and type IIR bacteria

C Infection with type IIR bacteria

D Infection with type IIIS bacteria

E All of the above

CM55 ___ This is the coding strand of DNA. Which of the following is the template?

5' - ATCATATTGGCG - 3'

A 5' - CGCCTTATTGAT - 3' D 5' - TAGTATAACCGC - 3'

B 5' - AUCAUAUUGGCG - 3' E 3' - TUCTUTUUCCGC - 5'

C 3' - TAGTATAACCGC - 5'

CM56 ___ This is the Template strand of DNA. Which of the following is the coding strand?

3' - ATCATATTGGCG - 5'

A 3' - TUCTUTUUCCGC - 5' D 5' - TAGTATAACCGC - 3'

B 5' - AUCAUAUUGGCG - 3' E 5' - CGCCTTATTGAT - 3'

C 3' - TAGTATAACCGC - 5'

CM57 ___ This is the coding strand of DNA. Which of the following is the mRNA sequence?

5' - ATCATATTGGCG - 3'

A 3' - TUCTUTUUCCGC - 5' D 5' - TAGTATAACCGC - 3'

B 5' - AUCAUAUUGGCG - 3' E 5' - CGCCTTATTGAT - 3'

C 3' - TAGTATAACCGC - 5'

CM58 ___ This is the mRNA sequence. Which of the following is the coding?

5' - AUCAUAUUGGCG - 3'

A 5' - CGCCTTATTGAT - 3' D 5' - TAGTATAACCGC - 3'

B 5' - ATCATATTGGCG - 3' E 3' - TUCTUTUUCCGC - 5'

C 3' - TAGTATAACCGC - 5'

CM59 ___ The process in which each strand of DNA separates and each is used as a template to create a new double-stranded DNA molecule

A Semi-conservative replication D Initiation

B Transcription E None of the above

C Translation

CM60 ___ The process in which each strand of DNA separates and each is used as a template to create a new double-stranded DNA molecule

A Transcription D Initiation

B Polymerase Chain Reaction E None of the above

C Translation

14

CM61 ____ The process in which each strand of DNA separates and each is used as a template to create a new double-stranded DNA molecule
A   Translation   D   Initiation
B   Transcription   E   None of the above
C   Replication

CM62 ____ The process in which each strand of DNA separates and each is used as a template to create a new double-stranded DNA molecule
A   Polymerase Chain Reaction   D   All of the above (A-C)
B   Semi-conservative replication   E   None of the above
C   Replication

CM63 ____ Which of the following molecules will be translated?
A   mRNA   D   siRNA
B   rRNA   E   tRNA
C   microRNA

CM64 ____ Which of the following molecules are used in the translation process?
A   RNA polymerase   D   siRNA
B   rRNA   E   All are used
C   microRNA

CM65 ____ Which of the following molecules will be used in the translation process?
A   mRNA   D   siRNA
B   DNA polymerase   E   tRNA
C   microRNA

CM66 ____ These operons are typically catabolic in nature
A   Inducible operons   D   *up* operons
B   Repressible operons   E   *down* operons
C   *lac* operons

CM67 ____ These operons are typically anabolic in nature
A   Inducible operons   D   *up* operons
B   Repressible operons   E   *down* operons
C   *lac* operons

CM68 ____ The temperature required to separate two complementary strands of the same DNA molecule is affected by which of the following factors?
A   The G/T content of the strand   D   The availability of DNA helicase
B   The direction of the strand   E   The availability of DNA polymerase
C   The G/C content of the strand

CM69 ____ The temperature required to separate two complementary strands of the same DNA molecule is affected by which of the following factors?
A   The A/T content of the strand   D   The availability of DNA helicase
B   The direction of the strand   E   The availability of DNA polymerase
C   The G/T content of the strand

CM70 ____ Which of the following molecules is NOT required for DNA replication in a cell?
A   DNA polymerase   D   Single stranded binding proteins
B   Topoisomerase   E   all are required for DNA replication in a cell
C   Helicase

CM71 ___ Which of the following molecules is NOT required for DNA replication in a cell?
  A RNA polymerase   D Single stranded binding proteins
  B Topoisomerase   E all are required for DNA replication in a cell
  C Helicase

CM72 ___ Which of the following molecules is NOT required for DNA replication in a cell?
  A DNA polymerase   D Single stranded binding proteins
  B tRNA   E all are required for DNA replication in a cell
  C Helicase

CM73 ___ The part of a tRNA that holds an amino acid when "charged"
  A Magnetic arm   D Holder-arm
  B Anti-codon sequence   E None of the above
  C Acceptor arm

CM74 ___ The part of a tRNA that binds to an mRNA
  A Magnetic arm   D Holder-arm
  B Anti-codon sequence   E None of the above
  C Acceptor arm

CM75 ___ When a polypeptide, a coding sequence and an mRNA are all read in the same direction
  A Complementary base pairing   D Transcription/translation stability
  B Co-linearity of gene expression   E None of the above
  C Polymerase gene order

CM76 ___ The most prevalent cancer type in Humans is found in:
  A Bone cells   D Nerve cells
  B Blood cells   E None of the above
  C Epithelial cells

CM77 ___ A group of cells that carry a mutation that causes unchecked cell growth but do not move from their initial tissue location.
  A Malignant cancer cells   D Un-methylated cancer cells
  B Benign cancer cells   E None of the above
  C Methylated cancer cells

CM78 ___ A group of cells that carry a mutation that causes unchecked cell growth and are found away from their initial tissue location.
  A Malignant cancer cells   D Un-methylated cancer cells
  B Benign cancer cells   E None of the above
  C Methylated cancer cells

CM79 ___ A condition in which an *unusual* number of chromosomes are present
  A Euploid   D Aneuploid
  B Diploid   E None of the above
  C Haploid

CM80 ___ A condition in which a *normal* number of chromosomes are present
  A Euploid   D Aneuploid
  B Diploid   E None of the above
  C Haploid

CM81 ___ Human somatic cell chromosome composition
  A Euploid   D Aneuploid
  B Diploid   E None of the above
  C Haploid

16

CM82 ____ Human gamete cell chromosome composition
A   Euploid   D   Aneuploid
B   Diploid   E   None of the above
C   Haploid

CM83 ____ A mutation is located on chromosome 1q13.2. What does this mean?
A   The mutation is on the small arm of chromosome 1
B   The mutation is on the long arm of chromosome 1
C   The mutation is in the first gene of chromosome q
D   The mutation is in the 1st exon of the 13th gene on chromosome q
E   None of the above

CM84 ____ Which of the following is a fundamental requirement for microarrays?
A   Hybridization   D   Transcripts from an organism
B   An array of genes to be screened E   All of the above
C   Complementary base pairing

CM85 ____ Which of the following could be an effective comparison between two organisms?
A   The amino acid composition of orthologous genes
B   The amino acid composition of paralogous genes
C   The DNA composition of non-coding DNA sequences
D   The rRNA polypeptide sequences between the organisms
E   All of the above

CM86 ____ Over-lapping error bars indicate what in a figure?
A   That the samples cover a broad range of readings
B   That the samples may be equivalent
C   That the data is wrong
D   That the higher range is the better reading
E   All of the above

CM87 ____ Combines genomic and transcriptomic work to describe gene function
A   Comparative Genomics   D   Transcriptomics
B   Functional Genomics   E   None of the above
C   Proteomics

CM88 ____ Strives to understand the collection of RNA created from genes
A   Comparative Genomics   D   Transcriptomics
B   Functional Genomics   E   None of the above
C   Proteomics

CM89 ____ Investigates functional polypeptide networks
A   Comparative Genomics   D   Transcriptomics
B   Functional Genomics   E   None of the above
C   Proteomics

CM90 ____ Compares different organisms' DNA structure and features
A   Comparative Genomics   D   Transcriptomics
B   Functional Genomics   E   None of the above
C   Proteomics

CM91 ___ A study compares the expressed genes in an organism before and after a stimulus. This is an example of:

A   Comparative Genomics   D   Transcriptomics
B   Functional Genomics   E   None of the above
C   Proteomics

CM92 ___ A study compares the expressed genes between tthree organisms. This is an example of:

A   Comparative Genomics   D   Transcriptomics
B   Functional Genomics   E   None of the above
C   Proteomics

CM93 ___ It is 1985; you wish to study a particular prokaryote. Which technology would you to use?

A   Radioactive, four lane Sanger sequencing   D   Bioinformatics
B   Microsatellite diversity   E   All of the above
C   Single nucleotide polymorphisms (SNPs)

CM94 ___ It is 1995; you wish to study a several pea varieties. Which technology would you use?

A   Radioactive, four lane Sanger sequencing   D   Bioinformatics
B   Microsatellite diversity   E   All of the above
C   Single nucleotide polymorphisms (SNPs)

CM95 ___ It is 2005; you wish to study two different Human populations. Which technology would you be able to use?

A   Fluorescent Sanger sequencing   D   Bioinformatics
B   Microsatellite diversity   E   All of the above
C   Single nucleotide polymorphisms (SNPs)

CM96 ___ It is 2015; you wish to identify a prokaryotes via ITS DNA. Which technology would you be able to use?

A   Fluorescent Sanger sequencing   D   Transcriptomics
B   Microsatellite diversity   E   All of the above
C   Single nucleotide polymorphisms (SNPs)

CM97 ___ Which of the following is *least* likely to be random?

A   Four DNA base pairs matching four DNA base pairs in another sample
B   Four RNA base pairs matching four RNA base pairs in another sample
C   Three amino acids matching three amino acids in another sample
D   Ten DNA base pairs matching Ten DNA base pairs in another sample

CM98 ___ Which of the following is *least* likely to be random?

A   Four DNA base pairs matching four DNA base pairs in another sample
B   Four RNA base pairs matching four RNA base pairs in another sample
C   Three amino acids matching three amino acids in another sample
D   Six DNA base pairs matching Six DNA base pairs in another sample

CM99 ___ Which of the following is *most* likely to be random?

A   Four DNA base pairs matching four DNA base pairs in another sample
B   Four RNA base pairs matching four RNA base pairs in another sample
C   Three amino acids matching three amino acids in another sample
D   Ten DNA base pairs matching Ten DNA base pairs in another sample

CM100 ___ A common size for a polymerase chain reaction primer is 20 bp. How specific is this?

A   About One in a million   D   About One in One Hundred Billion
B   About One in One Hundred Million   E   About one in a Trillion
C   About One in a Billion

Central Dogma Sequence (CS)

CS1 Derive the missing mRNA strand. Indicate the 5' and 3' ends of your sequence

mRNA   __' - __ __ __ __ __ __ - __'

DNA Coding   __' - G C T C A T G - __'

CS2 Derive the missing Coding strand. Indicate the 5' and 3' ends of your sequence

DNA Coding   __' - __ __ __ __ __ __ - __'

DNA Template   __' - A T G C T C A - __'

CS3 Derive the missing mRNA strand. Indicate the 5' and 3' ends of your sequence

mRNA   __' - __ __ __ __ __ __ - __'

DNA Coding   __' - __ __ __ __ __ __ - __'

DNA Template   __' - A T C C A C A - __'

CS4 Derive the missing Coding strand. Indicate the 5' and 3' ends of your sequence

DNA Coding   __' - __ __ __ __ __ __ - __'

DNA Template   __' - C T T C G C T - __'

CS5 Derive the missing Template strand. Indicate the 5' and 3' ends of your sequence

mRNA   __' - U C G U C G U - __'

DNA Coding   __' - __ __ __ __ __ __ - __'

DNA Template   __' - __ __ __ __ __ __ - __'

CS6 Derive the missing mRNA strand. Indicate the 5' and 3' ends of your sequence

mRNA   __' - __ __ __ __ __ __ - __'

DNA Coding   __' - __ __ __ __ __ __ - __'

DNA Template   __' - A T G G T T A - __'

CS7 Derive the missing Coding strand. Indicate the 5' and 3' ends of your sequence

DNA Coding   __' - __ __ __ __ __ __ - __'

DNA Template   __' - C T T G C T A - __'

CS8 Derive the missing Template strand. Indicate the 5' and 3' ends of your sequence

DNA Coding   __' - T G C A A T C - __'

DNA Template   __' - __ __ __ __ __ __ - __'

CS9   Derive the missing mRNA strand. Indicate the 5' and 3' ends of your sequence

mRNA   __' - __ __ __ __ __ __ - __'
DNA Coding   __' - __ __ __ __ __ __ - __'
DNA Template   __' - A A C G T A G - __'

CS10   Derive the missing Template strand. Indicate the 5' and 3' ends of your sequence

mRNA   __' - U C A U A G C - __'
DNA Coding   __' - __ __ __ __ __ __ - __'
DNA Template   __' - __ __ __ __ __ __ - __'

CS11   Derive the missing Template strand. Indicate the 5' and 3' ends of your sequence

DNA Coding   __' - G C C T C G A - __'
DNA Template   __' - __ __ __ __ __ __ - __'

CS12   Derive the missing Coding strand. Indicate the 5' and 3' ends of your sequence

mRNA   __' - U C U A G C G - __'
DNA Coding   __' - __ __ __ __ __ __ - __'

CS13   Derive the missing mRNA strand. Indicate the 5' and 3' ends of your sequence

mRNA   __' - __ __ __ __ __ __ - __'
DNA Coding   __' - __ __ __ __ __ __ - __'
DNA Template   __' - G C T A T G G - __'

CS14   Derive the missing Template strand. Indicate the 5' and 3' ends of your sequence

mRNA   __' - U U C G C A U - __'
DNA Coding   __' - __ __ __ __ __ __ - __'
DNA Template   __' - __ __ __ __ __ __ - __'

CS15   Derive the missing mRNA strand. Indicate the 5' and 3' ends of your sequence

mRNA   __' - __ __ __ __ __ __ - __'
DNA Coding   __' - __ __ __ __ __ __ - __'
DNA Template   __' - A T T C A T G - __'

CS16   Derive the missing Template strand. Indicate the 5' and 3' ends of your sequence

DNA Coding   __' - T C A C T G C - __'
DNA Template   __' - __ __ __ __ __ __ - __'

U	UUU UUC	Phenylalanine F, Phe (4.0%)	UCU UCC UCA UCG	Serine S, Ser (7.0%)	UAU UAC	Tyrosine Y, Tyr (3.0%)
	UUA UUG				UAA UAG	STOP
					UGA	STOP
					UGG	Tryptophan W, Trp (1.3%)
	UGU UGC	Cysteine C, Cys (1.9%)				
C	CUU CUC CUA CUG	Leucine L, Leu (9.3%)	CCU CCC CCA CCG	Proline P, Pro (5.1%)	CAU CAC	Histidine H, His (7.8%)
					CAA CAG	Glutamine Q, Gln (3.7%)
					CGU CGC CGA CGG	Arginine R, Arg (5.3%)
A	AUU AUC AUA	Isoleucine I, Ile (5.7%)	ACU ACC ACA ACG	Threonine T, Thr (5.5%)	AAU AAC	Asparagine N, Asn (4.5%)
	AUG	Methionine M, Met (2.4%)			AAA AAG	Lysine K, Lys (5.4%)
					AGA AGG	
					AGU AGC	Serine S, Ser (7.0%)
G	GUU GUC GUA GUG	Valine V, Val (6.2%)	GCU GCC GCA GCG	Alanine A, Ala (8.6%)	GAU GAC	Aspartic Acid D, Asp (5.0%)
					GAA GAG	Glutamic Acid E, Glu (6.1%)
					GGU GGC GGA GGG	Glycine G, Gly (6.7%)

(START indicated at AUG)

Non-Polar	Polar	Aromatic	Basic	Acidic

CS17   Derive the missing single letter polypeptide sequence from the start codon.
Indicate the 5' and 3' ends.

Polypeptide   __' -   - __'

mRNA   __' - AUCUGAUGACC - __'

CS18   Derive the missing single letter polypeptide sequence from the start codon.
Indicate the 5' and 3' ends.

Polypeptide   __' -   - __'

mRNA   __' - UCAUGUCCGCA - __'

CS19   Derive the missing single letter polypeptide sequence from the start codon.
Indicate the 5' and 3' ends.

Polypeptide   __' -   - __'

mRNA   __' - _ _ _ _ _ _ _ _ _ - __'

DNA Coding   __' - T A T G C G A C T G C - __'

CS20   Derive the missing single letter polypeptide sequence from the start codon.
Indicate the 5' and 3' ends.

Polypeptide   __' -   - __'

mRNA   __' - _ _ _ _ _ _ _ _ _ - __'

DNA Coding   __' - _ _ _ _ _ _ _ _ _ - __'

DNA Template   __' - G T A C A C G T C G A - __'

Central Dogma Long Answer (CLA)

```
5'-GATGACAGTAGCTAGTCGATTGCTAGCTGATCGGGATGCTAGATCGAT-3'  PLUS (FRAMES 1-3)
3'-CTACTGTCATCGATCAGCTAACGATCGACTAGCCCTACGACCTAGCTA-5'  MINUS(FRAMES 4-6)

1 5'-GAT GAC AGT AGC TAG TCG ATT GCT AGC TGA TCG GGA TGC TAG ATC GAT-3'
2 5'-G ATG ACA GTA GCT AGT CGA TTG CTA GCT GAT CGG GAT GCT AGA TCG AT-3'
3 5'-GA TGA CAG TAG CTA GTC GAT TGC TAG CTG ATC GGG ATG CTA GAT CGA T-3'

4 5'-ATC GAT CTA GCA TCC CGA TCA GCT AGC AAT CGA CTA GCT ACT GTC ATC-3'
5 5'-A TCG ATC TAG CAT CCC GAT CAG CTA GCA ATC GAC TAG CTA CTG TCA TC-3'
6 5'-AT CGA TCT AGC ATC CCG ATC AGC TAG CAA TCG ACT AGC TAC TGT CAT C-3'
```

CLA1 Knowing that UAA, UAG and UGA are stop codons, which of the above sequences represents an open reading frame?

CLA2 List five central dogma molecules that carry out their function in the nucleus

CLA3 List five central dogma molecules that carry out their function in the cytoplasm

Use the following abstrract to answer questions CLA4-7.

PLoS Biol 2008: 6(5): e108. doi:10.1371/journal.pbio.0060108 (open access)

Allele-Specific Up-Regulation of FGFR2 Increases Susceptibility to Breast Cancer

Kerstin B. Meyer, Ana-Teresa Maia, Martin O'Reilly, Andrew E. Teschendorff, Suet-Feung Chin, Carlos Caldas, Bruce A. J. Ponder

The recent whole-genome scan for breast cancer has revealed the FGFR2 (fibroblast growth factor receptor 2) gene as a locus associated with a small, but highly significant, increase in the risk of developing breast cancer. Using fine-scale genetic mapping of the region, it has been possible to narrow the causative locus to a haplotype of eight strongly linked single nucleotide polymorphisms (SNPs) spanning a region of 7.5 kilobases (kb) in the second intron of the FGFR2 gene. Here we describe a functional analysis to define the causative SNP, and we propose a model for a disease mechanism. Using gene expression microarray data, we observed a trend of increased FGFR2 expression in the rare homozygotes. This trend was confirmed using real-time (RT) PCR, with the difference between the rare and the common homozygotes yielding a Wilcox p-value of 0.028. To elucidate which SNPs might be responsible for this difference, we examined protein–DNA interactions for the eight most strongly disease-associated SNPs in different breast cell lines. We identify two cis-regulatory SNPs that alter binding affinity for transcription factors Oct-1/Runx2 and C/EBPb, and we demonstrate that both sites are occupied in vivo. In transient transfection experiments, the two SNPs can synergize giving rise to increased FGFR2 expression. We propose a model in which the Oct-1/Runx2 and C/EBPb binding sites in the disease-associated allele are able to lead to an increase in FGFR2 gene expression, thereby increasing the propensity for tumour formation.

CLA4 What is the problem they want to solve?

CLA5 What is their testable hypothesis?

CLA6 Describe their controlled experiment:

CLA7 What data did they collect (you will have to look up the full manuscript)?

CLA8 Draw prokaryote and eukaryote replication forks. Identify what is different about the two different processes.

CLA9 Using the first generation sanger sequencing gel at right, draw where the bands would be for the sequence 5' - ATGCTATAG - 3'

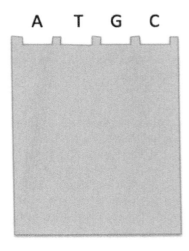

CLA10 Calculate the odds (in fractions) of encountering the sequence 5' - ATACGA - 3' in a random fragment of DNA.

CLA11 Calculate the odds (in fractions) of encountering the sequence 5' - GGCC - 3' in a random fragment of DNA.

CLA12 A mutation in the first base pair of the anti-codon sequence in the sole prokaryote proline tRNA gene has occurred, changing it to recognize serine codons. What are two likely effects that this will have for the organism?

CLA13 Calculate the odds (in fractions) of encountering the sequence 5' - PRNL - 3' in a random polypeptide

Genome Biology 2015, 16:171

Graded gene expression changes determine phenotype severity in mouse models of CRX-associated retinopathies

Philip A. Ruzycki, Nicholas M. Tran, Vladimir J. Kefalov, Alexander V. Kolesnikov and Shiming Chen

Background
Mutations in the cone-rod-homeobox protein CRX are typically associated with dominant blinding retinopathies with variable age of onset and severity. Five well-characterized mouse models carrying different Crx mutations show a wide range of disease phenotypes. To determine if the phenotype variability correlates with distinct changes in CRX target gene expression, we perform RNA-seq analyses on three of these models and compare the results with published data.

Results
Despite dramatic phenotypic differences between the three models tested, graded expression changes in shared sets of genes are detected. Phenotype severity correlates with the down-regulation of genes encoding key rod and cone phototransduction proteins. Interestingly, in increasingly severe mouse models, the transcription of many rod-enriched genes decreases decrementally, whereas that of cone-enriched genes increases incrementally. Unlike down-regulated genes, which show a high degree of CRX binding and dynamic epigenetic profiles in normal retinas, the up-regulated cone-enriched genes do not correlate with direct activity of CRX, but instead likely reflect a change in rod cell-fate integrity. Furthermore, these analyses describe the impact of minor gene expression changes on the phenotype, as two mutants showed marginally distinguishable expression patterns but huge phenotypic differences, including distinct mechanisms of retinal degeneration.

Conclusions
Our results implicate a threshold effect of gene expression level on photoreceptor function and survival, highlight the importance of CRX in photoreceptor subtype development and maintenance, and provide a molecular basis for phenotype variability in CRX-associated retinopathies.

CLA14 What is the problem they want to solve?

CLA15 What is their testable hypothesis?

CLA16 Describe their controlled experiment

CLA17 What data did they collect?

CLA18 What were their conclusions?

Transmission Genetics True/False (TTF)

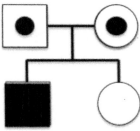

TTF1 ____ The pedigree above represents possible Autosomal Recessive Inheritance (Carriers Shown)

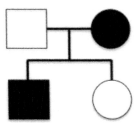

TTF2 ____ The pedigree above represents possible Autosomal Dominant Inheritance

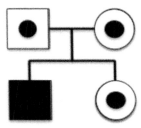

TTF3 ____ The pedigree above represents possible Autosomal Recessive Inheritance (Carriers Shown)

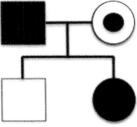

TTF4 ____ The pedigree above represents possible Autosomal Recessive Inheritance (Carriers Shown)

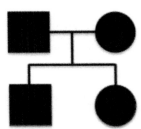

TTF5 ____ The pedigree above represents possible Autosomal Recessive Inheritance

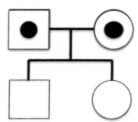

TTF6 ___   The pedigree above represents possible Autosomal Recessive Inheritance (Carriers Shown)

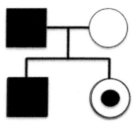

TTF7 ___   The pedigree above represents possible Autosomal Recessive Inheritance (Carriers Shown)

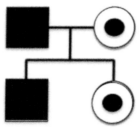

TTF8 ___   The pedigree above represents possible Autosomal Recessive Inheritance (Carriers Shown)

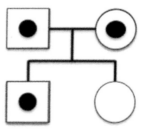

TTF9 ___   The pedigree above represents possible Autosomal Recessive Inheritance (Carriers Shown)

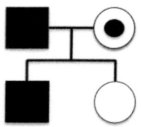

TTF10 ___   The pedigree above represents possible Autosomal Dominant Inheritance

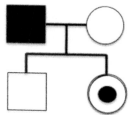

TTF11 ____   The pedigree above represents possible Autosomal Recessive Inheritance (Carriers Shown)

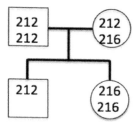

TTF12 ____   The pedigree above represents possible Simple Sequence Repeat (SSR) Inheritance

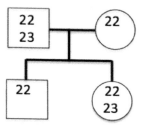

TTF13 ____   The pedigree above represents Single Nucleotide Polymorphism (SNP) Inheritance

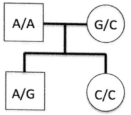

TTF14 ____   The pedigree above represents possible Simple Sequence Repeat (SSR) Inheritance

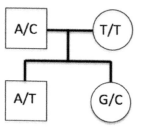

TTF15 ____   The pedigree above represents Single Nucleotide Polymorphism (SNP) Inheritance

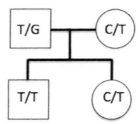

TTF16 ____   The pedigree above represents Single Nucleotide Polymorphism (SNP) Inheritance

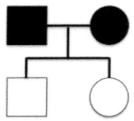

TTF17 ____   The pedigree above represents possible Autosomal Dominant Inheritance

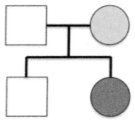

TTF18 ____   The pedigree above represents possible Mitochondrial Inheritance

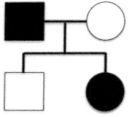

TTF19 ____   The pedigree above represents possible Simple Sequence Repeat (SSR) Inheritance

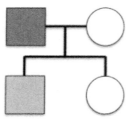

TTF20 ____   The pedigree above represents possible Mitochondrial Inheritance

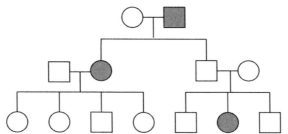

TTF21 ___ The pedigree above represents possible autosomal recessive inheritance (carriers not shown)

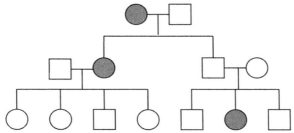

TTF22 ___ The pedigree above represents possible autosomal dominant inheritance

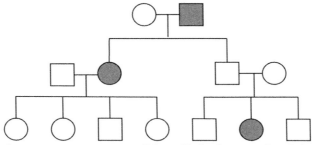

TTF23 ___ The pedigree above represents possible x-linked recessive inheritance (carriers not shown)

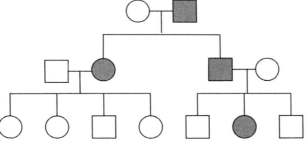

TTF24 ___ The pedigree above represents possible x-linked dominant inheritance

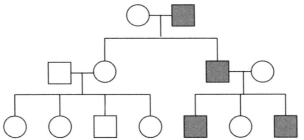

TTF25 ___ The pedigree above represents possible y-linked inheritance

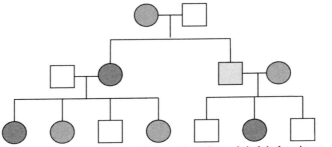

TTF26 ____   The pedigree above represents possible Mitochondrial inheritance

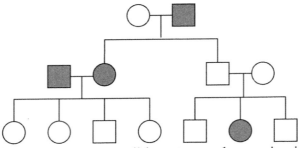

TTF27 ____   The pedigree above represents possible autosomal recessive inheritance (carriers not shown)

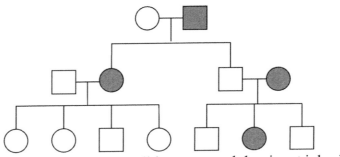

TTF28 ____   The pedigree above represents possible autosomal dominant inheritance

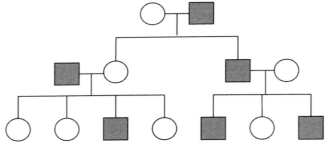

TTF29 ____   The pedigree above represents possible Y-linked Inheritance

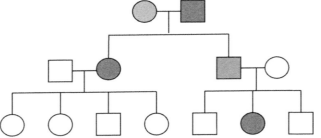

TTF30 ____   The pedigree above represents possible Mitochondrial Inheritance

TM1 ____ You are treating a family that has Huntingtons disease. You obtain sequence from the HTT gene for each affected family member and notice that the younger members of the family are presenting the disease earlier than their older relatives. What repeat-based phenomenon could explain this?

A	Mono-genic inheritance	D	An induced transcription factor
B	Trisomy	E	Anticipation
C	Defective (Recessive) allele		

TM2 ____ You have a child. This child's fingers are longer than you or your spouse/other biological parent. What is the likely reason?

A	Heterosis	D	Smart chromosome Trisomy
B	Incomplete dominance	E	None of the Above
C	Massive Mendelian Inheritance		

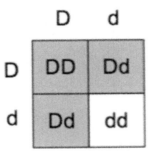

TM3 ____ What type of inheritance is indicated in this Punnett square?

A	Heterosis	D	Autosomal Recessive
B	Incomplete Dominance	E	None of the Above
C	Y-linked		

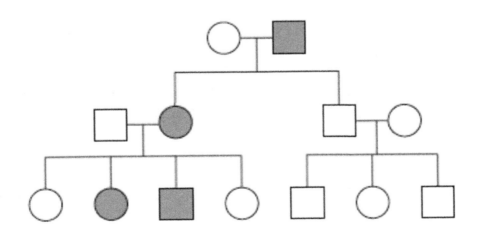

TM4 ____ What type of inheritance is indicated in this pedigree (ALL CARRIERS ARE SHOWN)?

A	Autosomal recessive	D	X-Linked Recessive
B	Mitochondrial	E	None of the Above
C	X-linked Dominant		

TM5 ___ Mendel crossed homozygous parents with smooth (SS) and wrinkled (ss) seed to make heterozygous smooth F1 seed. These F1 seed were then selfed. What is the chance that an F1 seed chosen at random will be wrinkled?

A 75% D 66%
B 25% E 0%
C 33%

TM6 ___ Mendel crossed homozygous parents with smooth (SS) and wrinkled (ss) seed to make heterozygous smooth F1 seed. These F1 seed were then selfed. What is the chance that a wrinkled F2 seed will produce smooth seeds when selfed?

A 75% D 66%
B 25% E 0%
C 33%

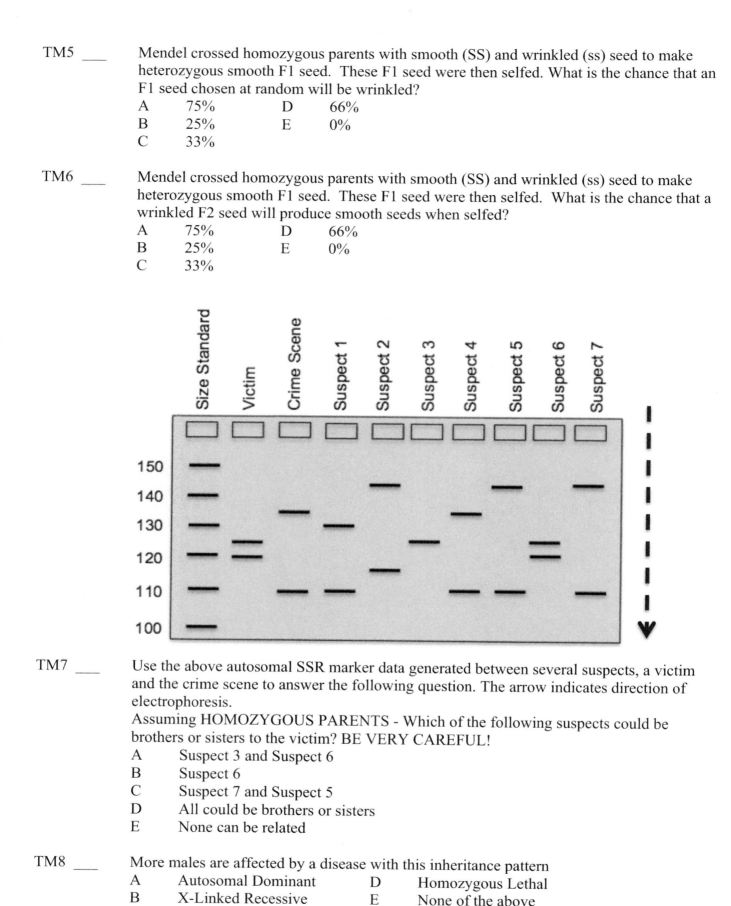

TM7 ___ Use the above autosomal SSR marker data generated between several suspects, a victim and the crime scene to answer the following question. The arrow indicates direction of electrophoresis.
Assuming HOMOZYGOUS PARENTS - Which of the following suspects could be brothers or sisters to the victim? BE VERY CAREFUL!

A Suspect 3 and Suspect 6
B Suspect 6
C Suspect 7 and Suspect 5
D All could be brothers or sisters
E None can be related

TM8 ___ More males are affected by a disease with this inheritance pattern

A Autosomal Dominant D Homozygous Lethal
B X-Linked Recessive E None of the above
C X-Linked Dominant

32

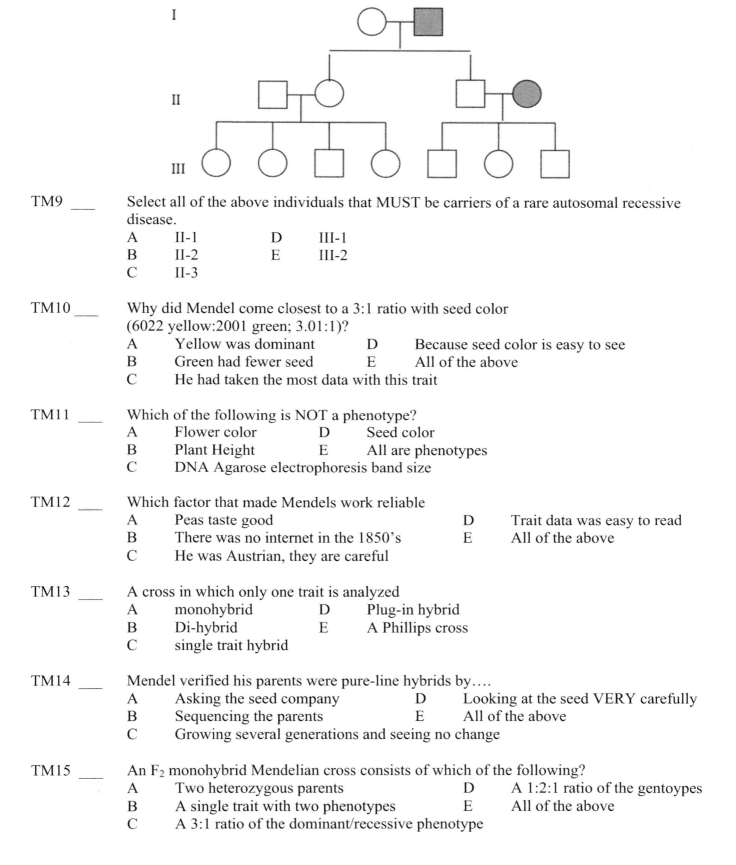

TM9 ___ Select all of the above individuals that MUST be carriers of a rare autosomal recessive disease.
A   II-1   D   III-1
B   II-2   E   III-2
C   II-3

TM10 ___ Why did Mendel come closest to a 3:1 ratio with seed color (6022 yellow:2001 green; 3.01:1)?
A   Yellow was dominant   D   Because seed color is easy to see
B   Green had fewer seed   E   All of the above
C   He had taken the most data with this trait

TM11 ___ Which of the following is NOT a phenotype?
A   Flower color   D   Seed color
B   Plant Height   E   All are phenotypes
C   DNA Agarose electrophoresis band size

TM12 ___ Which factor that made Mendels work reliable
A   Peas taste good   D   Trait data was easy to read
B   There was no internet in the 1850's   E   All of the above
C   He was Austrian, they are careful

TM13 ___ A cross in which only one trait is analyzed
A   monohybrid   D   Plug-in hybrid
B   Di-hybrid   E   A Phillips cross
C   single trait hybrid

TM14 ___ Mendel verified his parents were pure-line hybrids by….
A   Asking the seed company   D   Looking at the seed VERY carefully
B   Sequencing the parents   E   All of the above
C   Growing several generations and seeing no change

TM15 ___ An F_2 monohybrid Mendelian cross consists of which of the following?
A   Two heterozygous parents   D   A 1:2:1 ratio of the gentoypes
B   A single trait with two phenotypes   E   All of the above
C   A 3:1 ratio of the dominant/recessive phenotype

TM16 ___   An F$_2$ Di-hybrid Mendelian cross consists of which of the following?
A   A 9:3:3:1 ratio of the dominant phenotype   D   Four heterozygous parents
B   A 1:2:1 ratio of the gentoypes   E   All of the above
C   A single trait with two phenotypes

TM17 ___   Di-hybrid crosses are useful for what?
A   Identifying nearness of genes (linkage) on a chromosome
B   Testing your ability to make an 8x8 Punnett square
C   Identifying disease inheritance patterns
D   Verifying paternity of children
E   All of the above

TM18 ___   What is a simpler way to perform a Mendelian test cross?
A   Cross your unknowns with a recessive control   C   Self the unknown, see results
B   Perform a genetic test on the unknown   D   All of the above

TM19 ___   Which of the following is NOT seen in autosomal recessive diseases?
A   Two unaffected parents   D   Heterozygote individuals are affected
B   The same frequency between sexes   E   All of the above are seen
C   2 Affected parents have 100% affected children

TM20 ___   Which of the following is NOT seen in autosomal dominant diseases?
A   Two unaffected parents   D   Heterozygote individuals are affected
B   The same frequency between sexes   E   All of the above are seen
C   2 unaffected parents have no affected children

TM21 ___   This inheritance pattern was not discovered by Mendel.
A   Mitochondrial   D   Quantitative/multifactorial
B   Sex-linked   E   None of these were discovered by Mendel
C   Lethal

TM22 ___   This inheritance pattern can only be identified by the lack of the recessive homozygote
A   Mitochondrial   D   Quantitative/multifactorial
B   Sex-linked   E   None of the above
C   Lethal

TM23 ___   This inheritance pattern can be identified by numerical-based traits
A   Mitochondrial   D   Quantitative/multifactorial
B   Sex-linked   E   None of the above
C   Lethal

TM24 ___   This inheritance pattern can be identified by environmental influence
A   Mitochondrial   D   Quantitative/multifactorial
B   Sex-linked   E   None of the above
C   Lethal

TM25 ___   This inheritance pattern can be identified by the lack of male carriers
A   Mitochondrial   D   Quantitative/multifactorial
B   Sex-linked   E   None of the above
C   Lethal

TM26 ___ Which of the following is NOT seen in X-linked recessive diseases?
A   Two unaffected parents   D   Heterozygote individuals are affected
B   The same frequency between sexes E   All of the above are seen
C   2 Affected parents have 100% affected children

TM27 ___ This inheritance pattern only affects one sex in Humans
A   Mitochondrial   D   Autosomal recessive
B   X-linked dominant   E   Autosomal dominant
C   Y-linked

TM28 ___ The most common X-linked disorder in Humans
A   Dwarfism   D   Swyer syndrome
B   Color-blindness   E   Down Syndrome
C   Hemophilia

TM29 ___ This inheritance pattern is only passed on from one sex in Humans
A   Mitochondrial   D   Autosomal recessive
B   X-linked dominant   E   Autosomal dominant
C   X-linked recessive

TM30 ___ This inheritance pattern creates a unique intermediate phenotype between the parents
A   Mitochondrial   D   Heterosis
B   X-linked dominant   E   Autosomal dominant
C   Incomplete dominance

TM31 ___ This inheritance pattern creates a heterozygous phenotype greater than the parents
A   Mitochondrial   D   Heterosis
B   X-linked dominant   E   Autosomal dominant
C   Incomplete dominance

TM32 ___ This technique introduces Cisgenic modifications into a genome (Indicate all that apply)
A   Backcross   D   Gene Gun
B   Agrobacterium   E   Polymerase chain Reaction
C   Lentiviruses

TM33 ___ This technique introduces Cisgenic modifications into a genome (Indicate all that apply)
A   Backcross   D   Gene Gun
B   Agrobacterium   E   All of the above
C   Lentiviruses

TM34 ___ This technique introduces Transgenic modifications into a plant genome (Indicate all that apply)
A   Backcross   D   Gene Gun
B   Agrobacterium   E   Polymerase chain Reaction
C   Lentiviruses

TM35 ___ This technique introduces Transgenic modifications into an animal genome (Indicate all that apply)
A   Backcross   D   Gene Gun
B   Agrobacterium   E   Polymerase chain Reaction
C   Lentiviruses

TM36 ___ This marker is primarily used to determine disease/carrier status

    A   SSR   D   Restriction fragment length polymorphism (RFLP)
    B   SNP   E   Microsatellite
    C   Classical

TM37 ___ This marker is primarily used to determine parental status

    A   SSN   D   Restriction fragment length polymorphism (RFLP)
    B   SNP   E   Microsatellite
    C   Classical

TM38 ___ This molecular marker is primarily used to determine crime scene presence

    A   SSR   D   Restriction fragment length polymorphism (RFLP)
    B   SNP   E   GPS
    C   Classical

TM39 ___ This molecular marker is detected using agarose electrophoresis

    A   SSR   D   Isozymes
    B   SNP   E   GPS
    C   Classical

TM40 ___ A CODIS fingerprint value of "15" means:

    A   There is a "15" chance of a match   D   There are 15 alleles
    B   There are 15 repeats in BOTH alleles   E   None of the above
    C   There are 15 individuals who match

TM41 ___ A CODIS fingerprint value of "15/18" means:

    A   There is a "15" chance of a match   D   There are 15 alleles
    B   There are 15 repeats in BOTH alleles   E   None of the above
    C   There are 15 and 18 individuals who match

TM42 ___ A CODIS fingerprint value of "245/259" means:

    A   There is a "245" chance of a match
    B   There are alleles with 245 and 259 repeats respectively
    C   There are 245 and 259 base pairs in the two alleles
    D   There are 245 alleles
    E   None of the above

TM43 ___ The above symbol means:

    A   Affected female   D   Carrier Male
    B   Affected Male   E   Consanguineous mating
    C   Carrier Female

TM44 ___   The above symbol means:
- A   Affected female
- B   Affected Male
- C   Carrier Female
- D   Carrier Male
- E   Consanguineous mating

TM45 ___   The above symbol means:
- A   Affected female
- B   Affected Male
- C   Carrier Female
- D   Carrier Male
- E   Consanguineous mating

TM46 ___   The above symbol means:
- A   Affected female
- B   Affected Male
- C   Carrier Female
- D   Carrier Male
- E   Consanguineous mating

TM47 ___   The above symbol means:
- A   Affected female
- B   Affected Male
- C   Carrier Female
- D   Carrier Male
- E   Consanguineous mating

TM48 ___   Indicates that a trait is controlled by two or more genes
- A   Polygenic
- B   Quasi-trait locations
- C   Multi-trait phenotype
- D   Hybrid Vigor
- E   All of the above

TM49 ___   Indicates that a trait is controlled by two or more genes
- A   Polynesian genetics
- B   Quantitative-trait loci
- C   Multi-trait phenotype
- D   Hybrid Vigor
- E   All of the above

TM50 ___   Indicates that a trait is controlled by two or more genes
- A   Polynesian genetics
- B   Multifactorial Trait
- C   Multi-trait phenotype
- D   Hybrid Vigor
- E   All of the above

TM51 ___ The trait controlled by Gene A is only seen when gene B has a dominant allele. This is an example of:

A   Hemizygous Gene A   D   Hypostasis of Gene A under Gene B
B   Epistasis of Gene A over Gene B   E   None of the above
C   Hypostasis of Gene B under Gene A

TM52 ___ Pigment of a flower is controlled by a single gene. there are three phenotypes: Black (BB), Grey (Bb) and white (bb). This is an example of:

A   Heterosis   D   Complete dominance
B   Hemizygous   E   Over-Dominance
C   Incomplete dominance

TM53 ___ In a normal distribution, what percent of readings fall within 1 standard deviation?

A   34%   D   95%
B   68%   E   99%
C   90%

TM54 ___ In a normal distribution, what percent of readings fall within 2 standard deviations?

A   34%   D   95%
B   68%   E   99%
C   90%

TM55 ___ In a normal distribution, what percent of readings fall within 3 standard deviations?

A   34%   D   95%
B   68%   E   99%
C   90%

TM56 ___ You are within 1 standard deviation of the average height for your sex. What percentage of the population is taller than you?

A   16%   D   95%
B   34%   E   99%
C   68%

TM57 ___ You notice that there are literally hundreds of known heterozygote parent pairs that have produced children in a population, but there are no homozygous recessive children. What does this indicate?

A   QTL allele   D   Hybrid Vigor
B   Lethal allele   E   Epistasis
C   Over-dominance

TM58 ___ Suppression of a maternal or paternal copy of a gene has been linked to:

A   Differentially Methylated Regions (DMRs)
B   Selective Methylation
C   Genomic Imprinting
D   Suppression of gene expression based on methylation
E   All of the above

TM59 ___ "Luck of the draw" inheritance is based on:

A   Random organelle segregation   D   Finding a rich spouse
B   Gambling during pregnancy   E   Genomic allele sorting
C   Nuclear Chromosome segregation

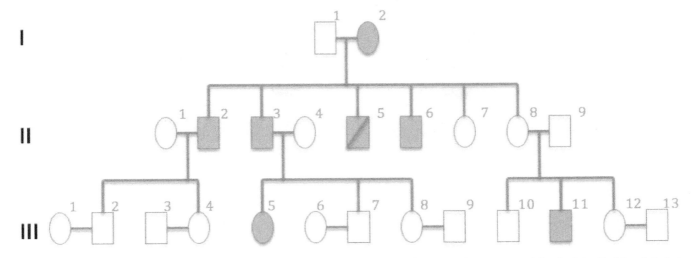

Answer questions TM60-TM64 using the x-linked recessive Disease Phenotype (shaded individuals) data and the disease genotypes that you can derive from the above pedigree.

TM60 ___ Which of the following must be a carrier?
A   II-2   D   III-3
B   III-1   E   Unable to determine
C   II-4

TM61 ___ Which of the following **must** pass on the disease allele to **all** of their female progeny?
A   II-4 and III-4   D   II-2 and II-3
B   I-2 and II-8   E   Unable to determine
C   I-2 and III-6

TM62 ___ Assuming II-1 is not a carrier, what percent of the male progeny from II-1 and II-2 will be carriers?
A   0%   D   75%
B   25%   E   100%
C   50%

TM63 ___ Using the provided and derived genotypes, what percent of the progeny from II-8 and II-9 will be carriers?
A   0%   D   75%
B   25%   E   100%
C   50%

TM64 ___ What percent of the progeny from III-5 would be affected assuming an unaffected mate?
A   0%   D   75%
B   25%   E   100%
C   50%

39

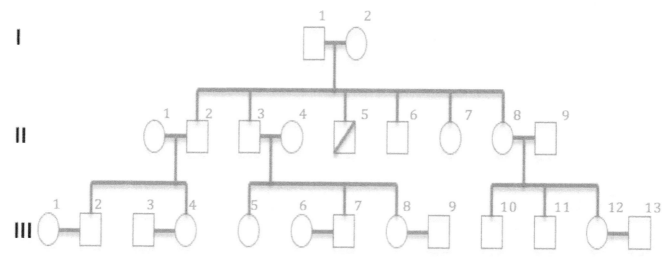

Starting genotypes: I-1 150/160; II-4 130/170; II-9 120/130; III-2 130/160; III-4 160/160; III-5 150/170; III-7 120/130; III-12 120/170

Answer questions TM65-TM70 using the following simple sequence repeat genotypes, complete (as far as you can) the pedigree above – You will have to derive several genotypes.

TM65 ____   Which of these is a possible genotype for II-2?
        A   140/120   D   160/120
        B   120/120   E   unable to determine
        C   130/120

TM66 ____   Which of these is a possible genotype for III-8?
        A   140/120   D   160/120
        B   120/120   E   unable to determine
        C   130/120

TM67 ____   Which of these is a possible genotype for II-8?
        A   170/120   D   170/150
        B   120/120   E   unable to determine
        C   130/120

TM68 ____   Which of these is a possible genotype for II-5?
        A   160/120   D   140/120
        B   120/120   E   unable to determine
        C   130/120

TM69 ____   Which of these is a possible genotype for II-1?
        A   160/120   D   150/120
        B   130/160   E   All are possible
        C   130/120

TM70 ____   Which of these is a possible genotype for III-10?
        A   170/120   D   170/140
        B   130/130   E   None are possible
        C   130/140

TM71 ___   Mendel crossed homozygous parents with Yellow (YY) and green (yy) seed to make yellow F_1 seed. These F_1 seed were then selfed. What is the percentage of seed in the F_2 generation that will be yellow?

A   0%   D   75%
B   25%   E   100%
C   50%

TM72 ___   Mendel crossed homozygous parents with Yellow (YY) and green (yy) seed to make yellow F_1 seed. These F_1 seed were then selfed. What is the percentage of seed in the F_2 generation that will be homozygous yellow?

A   0%   D   75%
B   25%   E   100%
C   50%

TM73 ___   Mendel crossed homozygous parents with Yellow (YY) and green (yy) seed to make yellow F_1 seed. These F_1 seed were then selfed. What is the percentage of seed in the F_2 generation that will be heterozygous yellow?

A   0%   D   75%
B   25%   E   100%
C   50%

TM74 ___   Mendel crossed homozygous parents with Yellow (YY) and green (yy) seed to make yellow F_1 seed. These F_1 seed were then selfed. What is the percentage of seed in the F_2 generation that will be heterozygous green?

A   0%   D   75%
B   25%   E   100%
C   50%

TM75 ___   Mendel crossed homozygous parents with Yellow (YY) and green (yy) seed to make yellow F_1 seed. These F_1 seed were then selfed. What is the percentage of seed in the F_2 generation that will be homozygous green?

A   0%   D   75%
B   25%   E   100%
C   50%

TM76 ___   Mendel crossed homozygous parents with Yellow (YY) and green (yy) seed to make yellow F_1 seed. These F_1 seed were then selfed. What is the percentage of seed in the F_1 generation that were homozygous yellow?

A   0%   D   75%
B   25%   E   100%
C   50%

TM77 ___   Mendel crossed homozygous parents with Yellow (YY) and green (yy) seed to make yellow F_1 seed. These F_1 seed were then selfed. What is the percentage of seed in the F_1 generation that were heterozygous yellow?

A   0%   D   75%
B   25%   E   100%
C   50%

TM78 ___ Mendel crossed homozygous parents with Yellow (YY) and green (yy) seed to make yellow F_1 seed. These F_1 seed were then selfed. What is the probability (in fractions) that an F_2 seed chosen at random **from among the yellow seeds** will breed true (produce only one phenotype) when selfed?

A 1/8 D 3/4
B 1/3 E All will breed true
C 2/3

TM79 ___ Mendel crossed homozygous parents with Yellow (YY) and green (yy) seed to make yellow F_1 seed. These F_1 seed were then selfed. What is the probability (in fractions) that an F_2 seed chosen at random **from among the green seeds** will breed true (produce only one phenotype) when selfed?

A 1/8 D 3/4
B 1/4 E All will breed true
C 2/3

TM80 ___ You cross homozygous pea plants with Tall (TT) and short (tt) height to make F_1 plants that are *taller than either of the parents*. These F_1 plants were then selfed. What is the percentage of progeny in the F_2 generation that are taller than either parent?

A 0% D 75%
B 25% E 100%
C 50%

TM81 ___ You cross homozygous pea plants with Tall (TT) and short (tt) height to make F_1 plants that are *taller than either of the parents*. These F_1 plants were then selfed. What is the percentage of progeny in the F_2 generation that are shorter than the F_1 plants?

A 0% D 75%
B 25% E 100%
C 50%

TM82 ___ You cross homozygous pea plants with Tall (TT) and short (tt) height to make F_1 plants that are *taller than either of the parents*. These F_1 plants were then selfed. What is the percentage of progeny in the F_2 generation that are the same height as the short parent?

A 0% D 75%
B 25% E 100%
C 50%

TM83 ___ A couple is concerned that a rare autosomal recessive disease occurs in both of their families. Tests confirm that they are both carriers for a SNP that causes this disease, in which the wild-type 'A' is mutated to a 'G'. What is the chance any child will be a carrier?

A 0% D 75%
B 25% E 100%
C 50%

TM84 ___ A couple is concerned that a rare autosomal recessive disease occurs in both of their families. Tests confirm that they are both carriers for a SNP that causes this disease, in which the wild-type 'A' is mutated to a 'G'. What is the chance any child will be affected?

A 0% D 75%
B 25% E 100%
C 50%

42

TM85 ___   A couple is concerned that a rare autosomal recessive disease occurs in both of their families. Tests confirm that they are both carriers for a SNP that causes this disease, in which the wild-type 'A' is mutated to a 'G'. What is the chance any child will not be a carrier or affected?

A	0%	D	75%
B	25%	E	100%
C	50%		

TM86 ___   A couple is concerned that a rare x-linked recessive disease occurs in the mothers family. Tests confirm that the mother is a carrier for a SNP that causes this disease. If they have a child, what is the chance they will be a carrier?

A	0%	D	75%
B	25%	E	100%
C	50%		

TM87 ___   A couple is concerned that a rare x-linked recessive disease occurs in the mothers family. Tests confirm that they are both carriers for a SNP that causes this disease. If they have a child, what is the chance they will be affected?

A	0%	D	75%
B	25%	E	100%
C	50%		

TM88 ___   A couple is concerned that a rare x-linked recessive disease occurs in the mothers family. Tests confirm that they are both carriers for a SNP that causes this disease. If they have a child, what is the chance they will *not* be a carrier or affected?

A	0%	D	75%
B	25%	E	100%
C	50%		

TM89 ___   In a cross between parent 1 AaBbCc x Parent 2 AaBbCc, what is the chance in fractions of having the genotype AaBbCc?

A	1/2	D	1/16
B	1/4	E	1/32
C	1/8		

TM90 ___   In a cross between parent 1 AaBbCc x Parent 2 AaBbCc, what is the chance in fractions of having the genotype AABbCC?

A	1/2	D	1/16
B	1/4	E	1/32
C	1/8		

TM91 ___   In a cross between parent 1 AaBbCc x Parent 2 AaBbCc, what is the chance in fractions of having the genotype aaBbCc?

A	1/2	D	1/16
B	1/4	E	1/32
C	1/8		

TM92 ___   This molecular marker type is the fastest growing and most common in humans

A	SNP	D	Microsatellite
B	SSR	E	Classical
C	RFLP		

TM93 ___ This molecular marker type is commonly used for human paternity testing
A   SNP   D   Microsatellite
B   SSR   E   Classical
C   RFLP

TM94 ___ This molecular marker type is commonly used for criminal investigations
A   SNP   D   Isozyme
B   SSR   E   Classical
C   RFLP

TM95 ___ This molecular marker type can be detected using electrophoresis
A   SNP   D   Microsatellite
B   SSR   E   All of the above
C   RFLP

TM96 ___ You wish to determine the genetic composition of an animal that is showing a dominant trait (B/?). You cross with another animal that shows the recessive trait (b/b). What is the genotype of the unknown if *All* of the 10 progeny show the dominant trait?
A   B/B   D   Either A or B
B   B/b   E   None of the above
C   b/b

TM97 ___ You wish to determine the genetic composition of an animal that is showing a dominant trait (B/?). You cross with another animal that shows the recessive trait (b/b). What is the genotype of the unknown if HALF of the 10 progeny show the dominant trait?
A   B/B   D   Either A or B
B   B/b   E   None of the above
C   b/b

TM98 ___ You wish to determine the genetic composition of an animal that is showing a dominant trait (B/?). You cross with another animal that shows the recessive trait (b/b). What is the genotype of the unknown if HALF of the 10 progeny show the dominant trait?
A   B/B   D   Either A or B
B   B/b   E   None of the above
C   b/b

TM99 ___ You wish to determine the genetic composition of an animal that is showing a dominant trait (B/?). You cross with another animal that shows the recessive trait (b/b). What is the genotype of the unknown if Half of the 4 progeny show the dominant trait?
A   B/B   D   Either A or B
B   B/b   E   None of the above
C   b/b

TM100 ___ You wish to determine the genetic composition of an animal that is showing a dominant trait (B/?). You cross with another animal that shows the recessive trait (b/b). What is the genotype of the unknown if ALL of the 4 progeny show the dominant trait?
A   B/B   D   Either A or B
B   B/b   E   None of the above
C   b/b

Transmission Genetics Pedigree (TP)

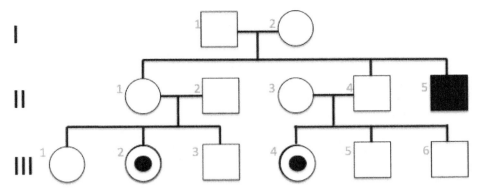

TP1   Indicate everyone who must be a carrier in the above RARE autosomal recessive pedigree

TP2   Assume II-5 finds a carrier mate. What percentage of their children will be carriers?

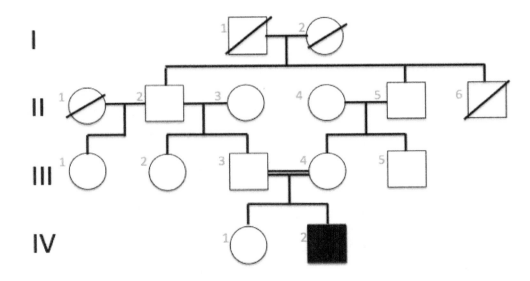

TP3   Who would you test in the above pedigree to see if they are carriers?

TP4   How could you determine whether I-1 or I-2 had been the carrier?

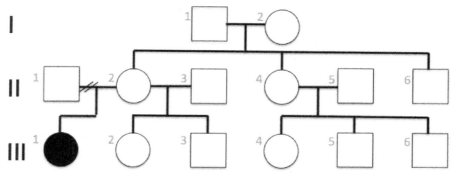

TP5 Who is the proband in the above autosomal recessive pedigree?

TP6 What is the relationship between II-1, II-2 and II-3 in the above autosomal recessive pedigree?

TP7 Who MUST be a carrier in the above autosomal recessive pedigree?

TP8 Who MIGHT be a carrier in the above autosomal recessive pedigree?

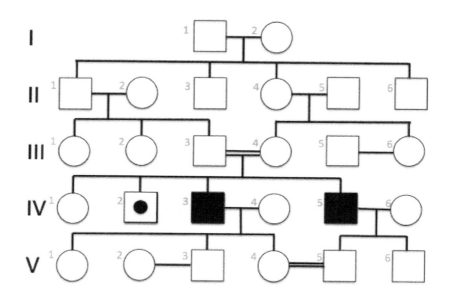

TP9 Who MUST be carriers in the above autosomal recessive pedigree

TP10 Who MIGHT be carriers in the above autosomal recessive pedigree

TP11 What century was generation I born in? (1800s, 1900s, 2000s) Why?

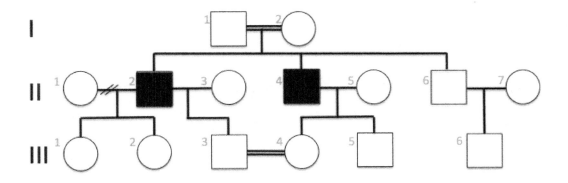

TP12 Who MUST be carriers in the above X-linked recessive pedigree?

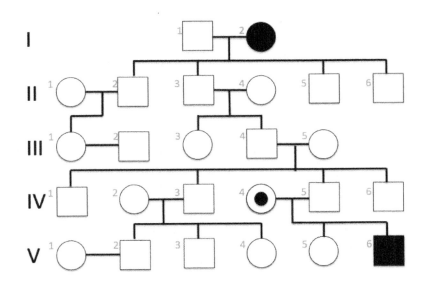

TP13   Who MUST be carriers in the above X-linked recessive pedigree?

TP14   Who MIGHT be carriers in this X-linked recessive pedigree?

TP15 Who MUST be affected in the above X-linked recessive pedigree?

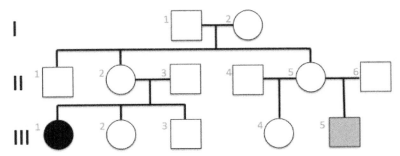

TP16 Who from the above mitochondrial pedigree would be affected?

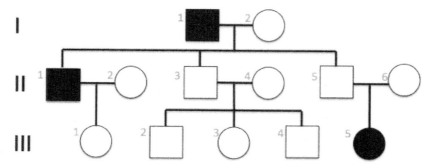

TP17 Who else in the above X-linked dominant pedigree must be affected?

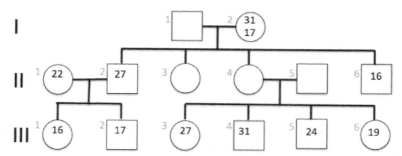

TP18 Complete as many genotypes as you can from the above pedigree (Homozygous SSRs indicated by 2 identical size entries)

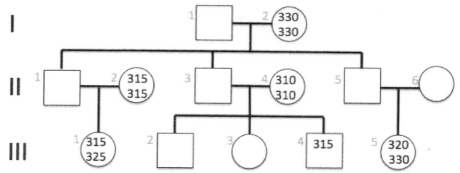

TP19 Complete as many genotypes as you can from the above pedigree (Homozygous SSRs indicated by 2 identical size entries):

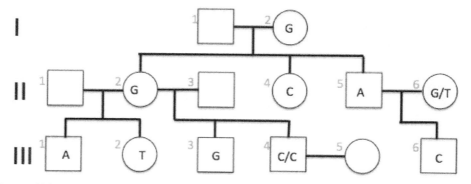

TP20 Identify all possible SNPs in the above Pedigree. I-1 and II-3 are homozygous. (Homozygous SNPs indicated by 2 identical nucleotide entries):

Transmission Genetics Long Answer (TLA)

Marker	Child 1	Child 2	Child 3	Product	Father 1	Father 2	Father 3
TPOX	216/220	227/237	220/237	216-264	220/220	216	227/260
D3S1358	99/147	99/112	147	99-147	130/147	130/147	112/134
FGA	158/300	246/300	300	158-314	158/300	158/314	246
D5S818	129/165	136/154	129/136	129-177	129/177	129/177	130/154
CSF1PO	316/320	312/320	320	287-331	316/320	287/320	294/312
D7S820	194/216	234/234	194/200	194-234	200/216	200	234
D8S1179	157/209	160/182	185/209	157-209	157/185	157/185	182/203
TH01	171/184	184	171/184	171-215	171	171/215	184/206
VWA	160	136/160	122/130	122-182	130/160	130	136/163
D16S539	156/280	129/177	129/349	129-177	280/349	129/349	163/177
D18S51	284/322	309/320	284/322	262-349	322	262/300	309
D21S11	164/272	194/242	180/242	154-272	180/272	180	194/235

Allele sizes reported in ascending order and do not indicate parental source. Product is the size range for the marker. Assume that the mother is the same for all three children.

TLA1 Based on the paternity data above, who is the father for child 1?

TLA2 Based on the paternity data above, who is the father for child 2?

TLA3 Based on the paternity data above, who is the father for child 3?

TLA4 Based on the identified fathers, what is the mothers genotype for TPOX?

TLA5 Based on the identified fathers, what is the mothers genotype for D5S818?

TLA6 Based on the identified fathers, what is the mothers genotype for VWA?

TLA7 If you have three siblings from two parents, how could you prove shared paternity (In other words, could you be sure that all three had the same father) without testing the parents?

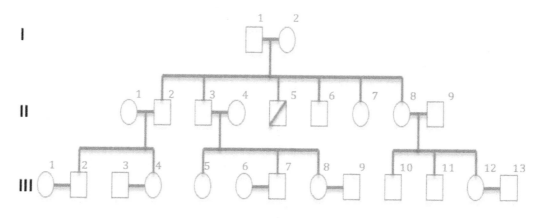

	SNP678*	SNP82451*	SSR*	Hair Color**
I-1	A	A/T	110	B-
I-2	A/T	C/G	110/113	B-
II-1	A	T	110/116	B-
II-2	A	T/G	110	B-
II-3	A/T	A/G	110/113	bb
II-4	A/G	A	116	B-
II-5	-	-	-	-
II-6	A	A/C	110/113	B-
II-7	A	A/C	110	B-
II-8	-	T/C	110/113	bb
II-9	T	G	107/116	bb
III-1	-	G/C	107/113	bb
III-2	A	G	110	Bb
III-3	T/G	C/T	110	Bb
III-4	A	T/G	110/116	Bb
III-5	T/G	A	113/116	bb
III-6	-	C/T	107/110	Bb
III-7	A/T	A	110/116	Bb
III-8	A	A	110/116	BB
III-9	A	A/C	110	Bb
III-10	A/T	T/G	107/110	bb
III-11	A/T	C/G	110/113	bb
III-12	A/T	C/G	110/116	bb
III-13	A/C	A	116	BB

*Detection method is capable of detecting all possible alleles
**Brown is dominant over blonde

TLA8   Among the already identified couples, who could be the parents of a child with SNP678(T/G), SNP82451(A), SSR(110/116), Hair color(bb)?

TLA9   Among the already identified couples, who could be the parents of a child with SNP678(A/T), SNP82451(T/G), SSR(107/113), Hair color(bb)?

TLA10 Among the already identified couples, who could be the parents of a child with SNP678(G/A), SNP82451(A/C), SSR(110), Hair color(bb)?

TLA11 Among the individuals in this population, who could be the parent of a child with SNP678(A/C), SNP82451(A/G), SSR(113/116), Hair color(BB)?

Population Genetics True/False (PTF)

PTF1 ___ No Mutation is a Hardy-Weinberg assumption (True/False)

PTF2 ___ No Random Mating is a Hardy-Weinberg assumption (True/False)

PTF3 ___ An insertion of 2 bp is more damaging in a gene than a deletion of 1 bp (True/False)

PTF4 ___ No Migration is a Hardy-Weinberg assumption (True/False)

PTF5 ___ An insertion of 3 bp is more damaging in a gene than a deletion of 1 bp (True/False)

PTF6 ___ No Natural Selection is a Hardy-Weinberg assumption (True/False)

PTF7 ___ An insertion of 1 bp is more damaging in a gene than a deletion of 3 bp (True/False)

PTF8 ___ A small population is a Hardy-Weinberg assumption (True/False)

PTF9 ___ An insertion of 3 bp is more damaging in an exon than a deletion of 1 bp in an intron (True/False)

PTF10 ___ An insertion of 1 bp is more damaging in an exon than a deletion of 23 bp in an intron (True/False)

PTF11 ___ Chromosome duplications are caused by non-disjunction (True/False)

PTF12 ___ Chromosome deletions are caused by non-disjunction (True/False)

PTF13 ___ A male inheriting a sex-linked trait is less likely to have problems than a female inheriting a dominant triat (True/False)

PTF14 ___ An autosomal chromosome deletion is more lethal than an autosomal addition (True/False)

PTF15 ___ Huntingtons disease is caused by a chromosome inversion (True/False)

PTF16 ___ A large number of mutations in a gene indicates that it is less likely to be central to the organisms survival (True/False)

PTF17 ___ A limited number of mutations in a gene indicates that it is likely to be central to the organisms survival (True/False)

PTF18 ___ Humans have a longer generation time than cats (True/False)

PTF19 ___ The wild-type allele is the most common allele in a population (True/False)

PTF20 ___ The Beneficial allele is the most common allele in a population (True/False)

PTF21 ___ A frameshift mutation removes a single codon and allows the polypeptide to continue growing (True/False)

PTF22 ___ A population of 100 people has 4 homozygous recessive affected individuals. This means there are 32 homozygous unaffected individuals in the population (True/False)

PTF23 ___ A population of 100 people has 4 homozygous recessive affected individuals. This means there are 32 heterozygous unaffected carriers in the population (True/False)

PTF24 ___ It takes four generations and consanguineous mating to see a new dominant mutation in a population (True/False)

PTF25 ___ PGD + IVF enable us to introduce non-carriers/unaffected children into our population (True/False)

PTF26 ___ The first person to write a book about Natural Selection was Alfred Wallace (True/False)

PTF27 ___ Macro-evolution has led to many new species (True/False)

PTF28 ___ Micro-evolution has increased diversity in Humans (True/False)

PTF29 ___ Migration into Europe occurred before migration into the Americas (True/False)

PTF30 ___ The world was populated only after we domesticated plants and animals (True/False)

Population Genetics Multiple Choice (PM)

PM1 ___ The portion of a phenotype that is caused by the environment is considered to be...

A Heritable D Central
B Transmittable E None of the above
C Migrational

PM2 ___ Which of the following are required for a population to be in genetic equilibrium (Multiple answers possible)?

A No Mutation D No Migration
B Survival of the Fittest E Central Dogma
C No Natural Selection

PM3 ___ Once a spontaneous dominant mutation has occurred in the progeny of a cross, it will become phenotypically evident at what time?

A When the affected individual mates with a sibling
B When the affected individual mates with a cousin
C When the affected individual mates with another affected individual
D In the progeny that inherited the dominant mutation
E All of the above

PM4 ___ A somatic-cell mutation has which of the following characteristics?

A All offspring are affected
B One parent must be a carrier
C Both parents must be carriers
D The condition cannot be transmitted to progeny
E The condition must be transmitted to male progeny

PM5 ___ A germ cell mutation that results in under-expression of many genes

A Chromosomal duplication D Sex Chromosome accumulation
B Autosomal dominant reversion E Chromosome deletion
C Sex Chromosome Y-linked inversion

PM6 ___ Disease A is autosomal recessive. A total of 16% of the study population of 100 people are affected. How many carriers are in the study population?

A 12 D 48
B 24 E 60
C 36

PM7 ___ Disease A is autosomal recessive. A total of 36% of the study population of 100 people are affected. How many homozygous unaffected individuals are in the study population?

A 16 D 64
B 32 E 80
C 48

PM8 ___ Identical twins were separated at birth. 34 years later, they found each other and were surprised that both of them were 5' 6" tall. This is an example of:

A Environmental influence D Mutation selection
B Natural selection E Reproductive success
C Heritability

PM9 ___ Worldwide, gene ABCD has an "R" amino acid in its polypeptide at position 64. The mutations p.R64T (53% of Asians), p.R64G (51% Europeans) mean which of the following could be relevant/true?

A   Founder-based mutation selection
B   A substantial number of individuals with a mutation
C   At least two different population based wild types
D   Migration-based wild types
E   All of the above

PM10 ___ A long-term study of Finches has been conducted on an island. After 192 generations, their progeny have separated into two distinct populations that are no longer able to create successful offspring between them and survive on different food sources. Why?

A   Macro-evolution   D   Micro-evolution
B   Natural selection   E   Environmental influence
C   Heritability

PM11 ___ The panels above indicate the effects of genetic drift on the heterozygosity of a single gene (starting at 50% each allele) through 50 generations of random mating. Indicate the smallest population to the largest based on maintained heterozygosity.

A   1,2,3   D   2,3,1
B   2,1,3   E   Unable to determine
C   3,1,2

PM12 ___ Which of the following sequences would result from the annotation c.72dupTA[4]? THINK CAREFULLY!

A   5' ...AUCACUAUAUAUACAGAUA..3'
B   5' ...ATCACTATACAGATA..3'
C   3' ...ATCACTATACAGATA..5'
D   5' ...ATCACTAATAATAACAGATA..3'
E   5' ...ATCACTAUATTACAGAUA..3'

PM13 ___ What is true of the "serial founder" effect?

A   All people of African descent are founders
B   All people from Europe are from a completely different gene pool
C   At each new founding event, genetic polymorphism is reduced in the new population
D   At each new founding event, genetic polymorphism is increased in the new population
E   None of the above are true

PM14 ___ Which of the following can cause mutation in Humans (multiple answers possible)?
- A Ionizing Radiation
- B Microwaves
- C Mutagenic Chemicals
- D Transposable elements
- E Spider bites

PM15 ___ The mutation annotation p.Leu231Thr indicates what?
- A The coding sequence at DNA bp 231 has been changed to a Threonine
- B The amino sequence at DNA bp 231 has been changed to a Threonine in a sequence
- C The amino acid at position 231 has been changed to a threonine in a polypeptide
- D The amino acid at position 231 has been changed to a stop codon in a polypeptide

PM16 ___ You are a carrier for a disease. You wish to remove any possibility that the disease allele will be transmitted to the next generation. Which of these can accomplish this (multiple answers possible)?
- A PCR
- B IVF+PGD
- C IVF only
- D Mating with an unaffected individual
- E Not having any children

PM17 ___ Indicate all that are Hardy-Weinberg Assumptions
- A No mutation
- B No migration
- C Random Mating
- D No National selection
- E All of the above

PM18 ___ Indicate all that are Hardy-Weinberg Assumptions (be careful!)
- A No Neutral Selection
- B Random meeting
- C No mitigation
- D No migration
- E All of the above

PM19 ___ Which of the following mutations is the most problematic for an organism?
- A 2 bp deletion in an intron
- B 3 bp deletion in an exon
- C 1 bp insertion in an exon
- D 6 bp deletion in an intron
- E Unable to determine

PM20 ___ Which of the following mutations is the least problematic for an organism (multiple answers possible)?
- A 2 bp deletion in an intron
- B 3 bp deletion in an exon
- C 1 bp insertion in an exon
- D 6 bp deletion in an intron
- E Unable to determine

PM21 ___ Which of the following mutations is the most problematic for gene A (3,846 amino acids l ong)?
- A 2 bp deletion in an intron
- B 2 bp deletion in the 236th exon
- C 1 bp insertion in the 3834th exon
- D 6 bp deletion in an intron
- E Unable to determine

PM22 ___ Which of the following mutations is the most problematic for an organism?
- A p.R146G
- B c.R146G
- C p.1384C>T
- D c.1384C>T
- E Either A or D

PM23 ___ Chromosome duplications are caused by:

    A   Non-disjunction   D   Orthologous Mutations

    B   Faulty Polymerase Chain Reaction   E   Paralogous Mutations

    C   Mom-disjunction

PM24 ___ A chromosome addition is caused by:

    A   Orthologous Mutations   D   Non-disjunction

    B   Faulty Polymerase Chain Reaction   E   Paralogous Mutations

    C   Nominal-disjunction

PM25 ___ Region A of a gene has significantly less mutations than region B of the same gene. What could cause this?

    A   The region is AT-rich   D   Region B is an intron

    B   The region is GC-rich   E   Unable to determine

    C   Region A is an exon

PM26 ___ Region A of a gene has significantly less mutations than region B of the same gene. What could cause this?

    A   Region A conserved due to necessary function   D   Region B is an intron

    B   The region is GC-rich   E   Unable to determine

    C   The region is AT-rich

PM27 ___ Allele A represents 60% of alleles in Human population 1, while allele B represents 54% in population 2. What can be said of this?

    A   Both Alleles A and B are Wild-types   D   B is the disease allele

    B   Allele A is the only Wild-type   E   All of the above

    C   A is the dominant allele

PM28 ___ A population of 1000 people has 40 individuals who are affected by an autosomal recessive disease. How many are homozygous unaffected?

    A   32   D   640

    B   256   E   810

    C   320

PM29 ___ A population of 1000 people has 40 individuals who are affected by an autosomal recessive disease. How many are heterozygous unaffected?

    A   32   D   640

    B   256   E   810

    C   320

PM30 ___ A population of 100 people has 4 individuals who are affected by an autosomal recessive disease. How many are homozygous unaffected?

    A   32   D   64

    B   26   E   81

    C   48

PM31 ___ A population of 20 people has 5 individuals who are affected by an autosomal recessive disease. How many are homozygous unaffected?

    A   5   D   20

    B   10   E   Unable to determine

    C   15

PM32 ___ A population of 20 people has 5 individuals who are affected by an autosomal recessive disease. How many are heterozygous unaffected?

A 5 D 20
B 10 E Unable to determine
C 15

PM33 ___ Domestication of plants and animals ocurred after…

A Humans migrated into Europe D Humans migrated from Africa
B Humans migrated into Asia E All of the above
C Humans migrated into North America

PM34 ___ Two healthy parents have nine healthy children, but their tenth child exhibits severe mental and physical issues. What is the most likely cause?

A Chromosomal Inversion D Chromosome 21 non-disjunction
B Autosomal Recessive disease E None of the above
C Autosomal Dominant disease

PM35 ___ Two healthy unrelated parents have three healthy children, but their fourth child exhibits severe mental and physical issues. What is the most likely cause?

A Chromosomal Inversion D Chromosome 21 non-disjunction
B Autosomal Recessive disease E None of the above
C Autosomal Dominant disease

PM36 ___ Two related, healthy parents have two healthy children, but their third child exhibits severe mental and physical issues. What is the most likely cause?

A Chromosomal Inversion D Chromosome 21 non-disjunction
B Autosomal Recessive disease E None of the above
C Autosomal Dominant disease

PM37 ___ Two unhealthy parents with similar symptoms have two unhealthy children with similar symptoms and one child that exhibits far more severe symptoms. What is the most likely cause?

A Chromosomal Inversion D Chromosome 21 non-disjunction
B Autosomal Recessive disease E None of the above
C Autosomal Dominant disease

PM38 ___ The portion of a phenotype that is caused by genes is considered to be...

A Heritable D Central
B Leaky E None of the above
C Migrational

PM39 ___ The un-inheritable portion of a phenotype is caused by…

A Genes D Environment
B SNPs E None of the above
C Classic genes

PM40 ___ Which of the following is not required for a population to be in genetic equilibrium?

A No Mutation D No Transportaton
B Random Mating E All are required for genetic equilibrium
C No Natural Selection

PM41 ___ Which of the following is not required for a population to be in genetic equilibrium?
A   No Mutation   D   No Migration
B   Random Mating   E   All are required for genetic equilibrium
C   No Natural Selection

PM42 ___ Once a spontaneous autosomal recessive mutation has occurred in the progeny of a cross, it may become phenotypically evident at what time?
A   When the affected individual mates with an unrelated individual
B   When the affected individual mates with a cousin
C   When the affected individual mates with another carrier
D   When progeny that inherit this mutation have consanguineous mating
E   All of the above

PM43 ___ Once a spontaneous chromosome addition has occurred in the progeny of a cross, it will become phenotypically evident at what time?
A   The effects will be immediately apparent
B   When the affected individual mates with a cousin
C   When the affected individual mates with another affected individual
D   In the progeny that inherited the dominant mutation
E   All of the above

PM44 ___ Once a spontaneous X-linked mutation has occurred in the male progeny of a cross, it will become phenotypically evident at what time?
A   The effects will be immediately apparent
B   When the affected individual mates with a cousin
C   When the affected individual mates with another affected individual
D   In the progeny that inherited the dominant mutation
E   All of the above

PM45 ___ A mutation that cannot be transmitted to progeny
A   Haploid cell mutation
B   Germ cell mutation
C   Somatic cell mutation
D   X-chromosome mutation
E   All mutations must be transmitted to progeny

PM46 ___ A condition that is not transmitted to progeny
A   Skin cancer
B   Mosaicism
C   Somatic cell mutation
D   Patau syndrome
E   None of the above can be transmitted

PM47 ___ A germ cell mutation that results in over-expression of many genes
A   Chromosomal duplication   D   Sex Chromosome accumulation
B   Autosomal dominant reversion   E   Chromosome deletion
C   Sex Chromosome Y-linked inversion

PM48 ___ A germ cell mutation that results in *mostly* normal expression of several genes, but may affect fertility

A   Chromosomal duplication   D Sex Chromosome accumulation
B   Autosomal dominant reversion   E Chromosome deletion
C   Chromosome inversion

PM49 ___ Which of the following sequences would result from the annotation c.1026dupGA[3]? THINK CAREFULLY!

A   5'...AUCACGAUAGAUACAGAUA..3'
B   5'...ATCACTATACAGATA..3'
C   3'...ATCCTCTCTGCTACAGATA..5'
D   5'...ATCACTAATAATAACAGATA..3'
E   5'...ATCACTAUATTACAGAUA..3'

PM50 ___ Which of the following sequences would result from the annotation c.72dupCAG[4]? THINK CAREFULLY!

A   5'...AUCACUAUAUAUACAGAUA..3'
B   5'...ATCACTATACAGATA..3'
C   3'...ATCACTATACAGATA..5'
D   5'...ATCACTAATAATAACAGATA..3'
E   3'...ATCAGTCGTCGTCGTCAUA..3'

PM51 ___ At each new event, genetic polymorphism is reduced in *two* populations.

A   Natural selection events
B   Bottleneck events
C   Random mating events
D   Serial founding events
E   None of the above are true

PM52 ___ At each new event, genetic polymorphism is reduced in *only one* population.

A   Migration events
B   Bottleneck events
C   Random mating events
D   Serial founding events
E   None of the above are true

PM53 ___ Which of the following can cause mutation in Humans (multiple answers possible)?

A   Ionizing Randomization   D   Transposable elements
B   Microwaves   E   All of the above
C   Mutagenic Chemicals

PM54 ___ Which of the following can cause mutation in Humans (multiple answers possible)?

A   Ionizing Radiation   D   Transposable elements
B   Replication errors   E   All of the above
C   Mutagenic Chemicals

PM55 ___ You are affected by an autosomal recessive disease. You wish to remove any possibility that the disease allele will be transmitted to the next generation. Which of these can accomplish this (multiple answers possible)?

A   PCR   D   Mating with an unaffected individual
B   IVF+PGD   E   Not having any children
C   IVF only

PM56 ___ You are male and affected by an X-linked recessive disease. You wish to remove any possibility that the disease allele will be transmitted to the next generation. Which of these can accomplish this?

A   PCR   D   Mating with an unaffected individual
B   IVF+PGD   E   Not having any children
C   IVF only

PM57 ___ You are female and affected by an X-linked recessive disease. You wish to remove any possibility that the disease allele will be transmitted to the next generation. Which of these can accomplish this?

A   PCR   D   Mating with an unaffected individual
B   IVF+PGD   E   Not having any children
C   IVF only

PM58 ___ The polypeptide for gene A is 1200 peptides long in brain tissue and 900 exons long in bone tissue. This is an example of:

A   Smart mRNA   D   Gene manipulation
B   Tissue engineering E   All of the above
C   Exon shuffling

PM59 ___ The polypeptide for gene A is 1200 peptides long in brain tissue and 900 exons long in bone tissue. This is an example of:

A   Smart mRNA   D   Alternative splicing
B   Tissue engineering E   All of the above
C   Intron reorganization

PM60 ___ The transcript for gene A is expressed equally in brain tissue and in bone tissue. This is a likely example of:

A   A housekeeping gene   D   Alternative splicing
B   Exon shuffling   E   All of the above
C   A specific transcription factor

PM61 ___ The transcript for gene A is expressed significantly more in bone tissue than in brain tissue. This is a likely example of:

A   A housekeeping gene   D   Alternative splicing
B   Tissue engineering   E   All of the above
C   A specific transcription factor

Population Genetics Allele Calculations (PA)

PA1   Disease A is autosomal recessive. A total of 16% of the study population of 100 people are affected. How many homozygous unaffected people are in the study population?

PA2   Disease A is autosomal recessive. A total of 16% of the study population of 100 people are affected. How many heterozygous unaffected people are in the study population?

PA3   Disease A is autosomal recessive. A total of 16% of the study population of 100 people are affected. How many unaffected people are in the study population?

PA4   Disease A is autosomal dominant. A total of 36% of the study population of 100 people are affected. How many homozygous unaffected people are in the study population?

PA5   Disease A is autosomal dominant. A total of 36% of the study population of 100 people are affected. How many homozygous affected people are in the study population?

PA6   Disease A is autosomal dominant. A total of 36% of the study population of 100 people are affected. How many heterozygous affected people are in the study population?

PA7   Disease A is autosomal recessive. A total of 91% of the study population of 100 people are unaffected. How many affected people are in the study population?

PA8   Disease A is autosomal recessive. A total of 91% of the study population of 100 people are unaffected. How many heterozygous carriers people are in the study population?

PA9   Disease A is autosomal recessive. A total of 91% of the study population of 100 people are unaffected. How many homozygous unaffected people are in the study population?

PA10   Disease A is autosomal recessive. A total of 1% of the study population of 100 people are affected. How many homozygous affected people are in the study population?

PA11   Disease A is autosomal recessive. A total of 1% of the study population of 100 people are affected. How many homozygous unaffected people are in the study population?

PA12   Disease A is autosomal recessive. A total of 1% of the study population of 100 people are affected. How many heterozygous unaffected people are in the study population?

Calculator Required
PA13   Disease A is autosomal recessive. A total of 0.005% of the study population of 100 people are affected (1 in 200 people). How many heterozygous unaffected people are in the study population?

PA14   Disease A is autosomal recessive. A total of 0.005% of the study population of 100 people are affected (1 in 200 people). How many homozygous unaffected people are in the study population?

PA15   Disease A is autosomal recessive. A total of 0.005% of the study population of 100 people are affected (1 in 200 people). How many unaffected people are in the study population?

PA16   Cystic Fibrosis is autosomal recessive. About 1 in 3,000 caucasians are affected (http://ghr.nlm.nih.gov/condition/cystic-fibrosis; 1/2019). What percent of the study population were homozygous unaffected?

PA17   Cystic Fibrosis is autosomal recessive. About 1 in 3,000 caucasians are affected (http://ghr.nlm.nih.gov/condition/cystic-fibrosis; 1/2019). What percent of the study population were heterozygous carriers?

PA18   Cystic Fibrosis is autosomal recessive. About 1 in 3,000 caucasians are affected (http://ghr.nlm.nih.gov/condition/cystic-fibrosis; 1/2019). What percent of the study population were unaffected?

Population Genetics Long Answer (PLA)

Use the following abstract to answer questions PLA1 - PLA3

PLoS Biol 5(5): e105.

A Dominant, Recombination-Defective Allele of Dmc1 Causing Male-Specific Sterility

Laura A. Bannister, Roberto J. Pezza, Janet R. Donaldson, Dirk G. de Rooij, Kerry J. Schimenti, R. Daniel Camerini-Otero, John C. Schimenti

DMC1 is a meiosis-specific homolog of bacterial RecA and eukaryotic RAD51 that can catalyze homologous DNA strand invasion and D-loop formation in vitro. DMC1-deficient mice and yeast are sterile due to defective meiotic recombination and chromosome synapsis. The authors identified a male dominant sterile allele of Dmc1, Mei11, encoding a missense mutation in the L2 DNA binding domain that abolishes strand invasion activity. Meiosis in male heterozygotes arrests in pachynema, characterized by incomplete chromosome synapsis and no crossing-over. Young heterozygous females have normal litter sizes despite having a decreased oocyte pool, a high incidence of meiosis I abnormalities, and susceptibility to premature ovarian failure. Dmc1, Mei11 exposes a sex difference in recombination in that a significant portion of female oocytes can compensate for DMC1 deficiency to undergo crossing-over and complete gametogenesis. Importantly, these data demonstrate that dominant alleles of meiosis genes can arise and propagate in populations, causing infertility and other reproductive consequences due to meiotic prophase I defects.

PLA1 The defective Dmc1 allele is located on an autosome, yet acts disproportionately against male vs female fertility. Describe the effect that this would have on the approximate 1:1 Male:Female ratio in a population.

PLA2 Describe a natural selection benefit to reduced meiosis that might explain propagation of the dominant defective allele.

PLA3 Design an experiment that would test whether a mouse population with defective Dmc1 alleles actually does produce equivalent progeny to a wild-type population of the same initial makeup.

Use the following abstract to answer questions PLA4 - PLA7

BMC Evol Biol. 2011; 11: 345.

Blackmailing: the keystone in the human mating system

Milind G Watve, Anuja Damle, Bratati Ganguly, Anagha Kale, and Neelesh Dahanukar

Background
The human mating system is characterized by bi-parental care and faithful monogamy is highly valued in most cultures. Marriage has evolved as a social institution and punishment for extra pair mating (EPM) or adultery is common. However, similar to other species with bi-parental care, both males and females frequently indulge in EPM in secrecy since it confers certain gender specific genetic benefits. Stability of faithful monogamy is therefore a conundrum. We model human mating system using game theory framework to study the effects of factors that can stabilize or destabilize faithful committed monogamy.

Results
Although mate guarding can partly protect the genetic interests, we show that it does not ensure monogamy. Social policing enabled by gossiping is another line of defense against adultery unique to humans. However, social policing has a small but positive cost to an individual and therefore is prone to free riding. We suggest that since exposure of adultery can invite severe punishment, the policing individuals can blackmail opportunistically whenever the circumstances permit. If the maximum probabilistic benefit of blackmailing is greater than the cost of policing, policing becomes a non-altruistic act and stabilizes in the society. We show that this dynamics leads to the coexistence of different strategies in oscillations, with obligate monogamy maintained at a high level. Deletion of blackmailing benefit from the model leads to the complete disappearance of obligate monogamy.

Conclusions
Obligate monogamy can be maintained in the population in spite of the advantages of EPM. Blackmailing, which makes policing a non-altruistic act, is crucial for the maintenance of faithful monogamy. Although biparental care, EPM, mate guarding and punishment are shared by many species, gossiping and blackmailing make the human mating system unique.

This manuscript discusses the concept that monogamy can be forced by societal pressure.
PLA4 Will this increase or decrease random mating? Why?

PLA5 How will this practice affect migration?

PLA6 How will this practice affect population size

PLA7 The following excerpt is from the same BMC manuscript. Find out what "resource partitioning" means in this context.

".......The human mating system is an ideal and obvious example of hidden strategy games. Since paternity is uncertain the actual reproductive success of a male remains hidden. For females although some of the components of benefits, for example resource partitioning and the number of offspring borne by them is obvious, the genetic contributor to the offspring and therefore the benefit of "good genes" remains hidden........"   BMC Evol Biol. 2011; 11: 345.

Use the following abstract to answer questions PLA8 - PLA10

PloS Biol 2(10): e286 (2004)

Population history and natural selection shape patterns of genetic variation in 132 genes.

Akey JM, Eberle MA, Rieder MJ, Carlson CS, Shriver MD, et al. (2004)

Abstract

Identifying regions of the human genome that have been targets of natural selection will provide important insights into human evolutionary history and may facilitate the identification of complex disease genes. Although the signature that natural selection imparts on DNA sequence variation is difficult to disentangle from the effects of neutral processes such as population demographic history, selective and demographic forces can be distinguished by analyzing multiple loci dispersed throughout the genome. We studied the molecular evolution of 132 genes by comprehensively resequencing them in 24 African-Americans and 23 European-Americans. We developed a rigorous computational approach for taking into account multiple hypothesis tests and demographic history and found that while many apparent selective events can instead be explained by demography, there is also strong evidence for positive or balancing selection at eight genes in the European-American population, but none in the African-American population. Our results suggest that the migration of modern humans out of Africa into new environments was accompanied by genetic adaptations to emergent selective forces. In addition, a region containing four contiguous genes on Chromosome 7 showed striking evidence of a recent selective sweep in European-Americans. More generally, our results have important implications for mapping genes underlying complex human diseases.

…Discussion….(partial, without citations)

TRPV6, as well as TRPV5, constitute the rate-limiting step in kidney, intestine, and placenta calcium absorption. Interestingly, Northern European populations have very high frequencies of the lactase persistence allele (LCT*P), which allows digestion of fresh milk throughout adulthood. It is widely accepted that strong selection has driven LCT*P to high frequency in Northern Europeans, beginning sometime after the domestication of animals approximately 9,000 y ago, What has been debated, however, is the specific selective advantage conferred by lactase persistence. Our finding that TRPV6 and/or TRPV5 have been under strong selective pressure in Northern Europeans suggests that increased calcium absorption may have been the driving force behind selection for lactase persistence. Although additional studies are clearly needed, our results provide additional insight into the molecular mechanisms of adaptation to a new dietary niche (i.e., high-lactose diets).

Lactose Phlorizin hydrolase (LPH; gene *LCT*) is an autosomal recessive gene. Describe how each of the following HW assumptions would affect its incorporation into a European population from 9,000 years ago until today.

PLA8 Random Mating:

PLA9 Migration:

PLA10 Genetic Drift:

Use the following abstract to answer questions PLA11 - PLA14

BMC Genetics (2015) 16:81

The role of climate and out-of-Africa migration in the frequencies of risk alleles for 21 human diseases

Lily M. Blair and Marcus W. Feldman

Background:
Demography and environmental adaptation can affect the global distribution of genetic variants and possibly the distribution of disease. Population heterozygosity of single nucleotide polymorphisms has been shown to decrease strongly with distance from Africa and this has been attributed to the effect of serial founding events during the migration of humans out of Africa. Additionally, population allele frequencies have been shown to change due to environmental adaptation. Here, we investigate the relationship of Out-of-Africa migration and climatic variables to the distribution of risk alleles for 21 diseases.

Results:
For each disease, we computed the regression of average heterozygosity and average allele frequency of the risk alleles with distance from Africa and 9 environmental variables. We compared these regressions to a null distribution created by regressing statistics for SNPs not associated with disease on distance from Africa and these environmental variables. Additionally, we used Bayenv 2.0 to assess the signal of environmental adaptation associated with individual risk SNPs. For those SNPs in HGDP and HapMap that are risk alleles for type 2 diabetes, we cannot reject that their distribution is as expected from Out-of-Africa migration. However, the allelic statistics for many other diseases correlate more closely with environmental variables than would be expected from the serial founder effect and show signals of environmental adaptation. We report strong environmental interactions with several autoimmune diseases, and note a particularly strong interaction between asthma and summer humidity. Additionally, we identified several risk genes with strong environmental associations.

Conclusions:
For most diseases, migration does not explain the distribution of risk alleles and the worldwide pattern of allele frequencies for some diseases may be better explained by environmental associations, which suggests that some selection has acted on these diseases

PLA11 What type of mapping is being performed?

PLA12 Write out the data that they would collect - what kind of form must the environmental data be in - and what does that tell you about the traits?

PLA13 What do you think they mean by "Out of Africa migration"?

PLA14 What do you think is meant by the "serial founder effect"?

PLA15 What do you think could cause the nearly worldwide diabetes distribution (which is reduced as distance from Africa increases), "Out of Africa" or the "serial founder effect"?

Laboratory-based questions (LAB)

LAB1 What are the four basic functions of a pipettor (4 pts)?

LAB2 Name 5 components of a PCR reaction (5pts)

LAB3 You have pipetted an unknown volume of water onto the scale, which reads

0.8738 g   How much have you transferred? _____ ul

LAB4 You have pipetted an unknown volume of water onto the scale, which reads

0.0034 g   How much have you transferred? _____ ul

LAB5 What would happen to the samples in the following PCR reaction?

Lid 93 °; Wait; Auto
95°   5 min
95 °   30 sec
40 °   60 sec
72 °   30 sec
Goto 2 Rep 40 times
72 °   5 minutes
Hold 4 °

Use the gel diagram below to answer questions LAB6-9 about the following *autosomal* gene
(P = parent, C = child)

Bp		P1	P2	C1	C2
1000	____				
		____	____	____	____
750	____				
500	____	____		____	
250	____				
100	____				

(Electrophoresis)

LAB6 Which parent is homozygous?

LAB7 This is a disease causing gene, with P1 and C2 showing the disease. What can you say about the ~900 bp allele? Is it the disease allele?

LAB8 Is the disease allele dominant or recessive?

LAB9 Which child is a *carrier* of the disease allele?

Use the gel diagram below to answer questions LAB10-14 about the following *x-linked* gene
(P = parent, C = child)

```
  Bp           P1    P2    C1    C2
 1000  ____
                   ____  ____  ____  ____
  750  ____

  500  ____   ____  ____        ____        (Electrophoresis)

  250  ____

  100  ____
```

LAB10   Which parent is the mother?

LAB11   This is a disease causing gene, with P2 and C1 showing the disease. What can you say about the ~900 bp allele? Is it the disease allele?

LAB12   Is the disease allele dominant or recessive?

LAB13   Which child is a *carrier* of the disease allele?

LAB14   Which allele in C2 came from the father and which allele came from the mother?

Multiple Choice

LAB15 ____   You have just run a PCR reaction in a thermal cycler. You attempt to load into an agarose gel but find that your PCR tubes are empty. What could be the cause?
    A   The components of the reaction ran out   D   You used the wrong pipettor
    B   The heated lid was not on   E   All of the above
    C   You forgot to put DNA into the reaction

LAB16   You wish to design primers with a high T_m. Which of the following sequences has the highest T_m?
    A   5' - CGCCTTATTG - 3'   D   5' - TAGTACAACC - 3'
    B   5' - ATCATAGGCG - 3'   E   3' - TCTTCCGCGT - 5'
    C   3' - TAGTATAACC - 5'

LAB17   You wish to design primers with a low T_m. Which of the following sequences has the lowest T_m?
    A   5' - CGCCTTATTG - 3'   D   5' - TAGTACAACC - 3'
    B   5' - ATCATAGGCG - 3'   E   3' - TCTTCCGCGT - 5'
    C   3' - TAGTATAACC - 5'

LAB18   The *Hind*III enzyme recognizes the following sequence 5'-AAGCTT -3'. Approximately how many times will it cut a random DNA sequence of 100,000 bp?
    A   4   D   25
    B   6   E   None of the above
    C   12

LAB19 The *Hae*III enzyme recognizes the following sequence 5'-GGCC -3'. Approximately how many times will it cut a random DNA sequence of 1,000 bp?

A   4   D   25
B   6   E   None of the above
C   12

LAB20 The genomic sequence of a gene is 10,000 bp long, the edited mRNA is 3,000 bp long and the polypeptide is 930 amino acids long. How many codons are in the edited mRNA?

A   2,790   D   6
B   930   E   Unable to determine
C   310

LAB21 The genomic sequence of a gene is 10,000 bp long, the edited mRNA is 3,000 bp long and the polypeptide is 930 amino acids long. How many base pairs are in codons?

A   2,790   D   6
B   930   E   Unable to determine
C   310

LAB22 The genomic sequence of a gene is 10,000 bp long, the edited mRNA is 3,000 bp long and the polypeptide is 310 amino acids long. How many codons are in the edited mRNA?

A   2,790   D   6
B   930   E   Unable to determine
C   310

LAB23 You wish to identify an unknown bacterial sample. Which database would be the most effective to search?

A   Standard non-redundant   D   Model
B   rna/ITS   E   Unable to determine
C   Human Genomic + transcript

LAB24 You wish to identify an unknown human gene sequence. Which database would be the most effective to search?

A   Standard non-redundant   D   Model
B   rna/ITS   E   Unable to determine
C   Human Genomic + transcript

LAB25 You wish to identify an unknown sequence sample. Which database would be the most effective to search?

A   Standard non-redundant   D   Model
B   rna/ITS   E   Unable to determine
C   Human Genomic + transcript

LAB26 Which of the following is a common danger in a molecular genetics laboratory?

A   Ethidium Bromide   D   Open flame
B   Poison   E   None of the above
C   Solar radiation

LAB27 Which of the following is a common danger in a molecular genetics laboratory?

A   Solar radiation   D   Open flame
B   Poison   E   None of the above
C   High Voltage

LAB28   This procedure results in fragments of DNA with specific ends
A   PCR   D   Pipetting
B   Colony PCR   E   Bioinformatics
C   Electrophoresis

LAB29   This procedure results in fragments of DNA with specific ends
A   DNA extraction   D   Pipetting
B   Restriction digest   E   Bioinformatics
C   Electrophoresis

LAB30   This procedure results in fragments of DNA without specific ends
A   PCR   D   Pipetting
B   Restriction digest   E   DNA extraction
C   Electrophoresis

LAB31   This procedure matches fragments of DNA without specific ends
A   PCR   D   BLAST
B   Restriction digest   E   DNA extraction
C   Electrophoresis

LAB32   You have designed a 10 bp PCR primer. How many random base pairs are needed to match this sequence?
A   10 bp   D   1,000,000,000 bp
B   1,000 bp   E   1,000,000,000,000 bp
C   1,000,000 bp

LAB33   You have designed a 15 bp PCR primer. How many random base pairs are needed to match this sequence?
A   10 bp   D   1,000,000,000 bp
B   1,000 bp   E   1,000,000,000,000 bp
C   1,000,000 bp

LAB34   You have designed a 20 bp PCR primer. How many random base pairs are needed to match this sequence?
A   10 bp   D   1,000,000,000 bp
B   1,000 bp   E   1,000,000,000,000 bp
C   1,000,000 bp

LAB35   Which of the following weighs more?
A   2.1 ml water   D   2,150 ul water
B   0.002 L water   E   5.002 nm
C   2.1 mg

LAB36   Which of the following weighs less?
A   2.1 ml water   D   2,150 ul water
B   0.002 L water   E   5.002 nm
C   2.1 mg

LAB37   The fire extinguisher is located:

LAB38   The number to call in an emergency:

LAB39   The first aid box is located:

LAB40   The eyewash is located:

LAB41   DNA runs to the negative (black) end of an electrophoresis gel (T/F)

LAB42   PCR stops when the template DNA is used up (T/F)

LAB43   DNA separation in PCR happens at 100° F (T/F)

LAB44   I should avoid skin contact with ethidium bromide (T/F)

LAB45   Genomic DNA includes introns (T/F)

LAB46   PCR doubles the amount of target DNA with each cycle (T/F)

LAB47   Detection of basic PCR is typically accomplished via some form of electrophoresis (T/F)

LAB48   In PCR, as cycle number increases, product quantity increases (T/F)

LAB49   One microliter of water equals one gram (T/F)

LAB50   DNA has a positive charge (T/F)

Answers

Central Dogma True/False (CTF)

CTF1	F	coding DNA and template DNA have wrong direction (5' - 3')
CTF2	T	
CTF3	F	U's in mRNA should be A's
CTF4	T	
CTF5	T	
CTF6	F	Third polypeptide should be cysteine (C); "UGU"
CTF7	F	mRNA has a "T"
CTF8	F	Coding DNA is reversed
CTF9	F	
CTF10	F	
CTF11	F	
CTF12	T	
CTF13	F	
CTF14	F	
CTF15	T	
CTF16	T	
CTF17	F	
CTF18	F	
CTF19	T	
CTF20	F	
CTF21	F	
CTF22	T	
CTF23	T	
CTF24	T	
CTF25	F	
CTF26	T	
CTF27	F	
CTF28	F	
CTF29	T	
CTF30	F	

Central Dogma Multiple Choice (CM)

CM1	A	Only mitosis is associated with DNA polymerase; meiosis II does not replicate DNA; Ribosomal polymerase reaction is a foil.
CM2	A	DNA polymerase is used for the replication of DNA (mitosis and meiosis I). All other molecules listed in this question are involved in translation.
CM3	B	The DNA template is used to make an RNA strand by RNA polymerase. microRNA is a functional RNA molecule, so there is no need to translate it
CM4	C	DNA polymerase is used to replicate DNA and is not involved in either transcription or translation.
CM5	D	RNAse is a substance that destroys RNA
CM6	A	microRNA anneals to an mRNA molecule and prevents it from being translated into a polypeptide
CM7	C	Ribosomes are associated with the conversion of mRNA to polypeptides - translation
CM8	C	RNA polymerase is involved in the transcription of DNA into RNA
CM9	C	siRNA anneals to an mRNA molecule and prevents it from being translated into a polypeptide
CM10	B&D	The PCR reaction uses heat to separate the two DNA strands, then DNA polymerase, primers and $MgCl_2$ are used to incorporate the nucleotides
CM11	D	Topoisomerase is used to unwind DNA and does not complementary base pair
CM12	D	Thermal cycler is a generic term for a PCR machine
CM13	A	no siRNA in prokaryotes, Gln-tRNA is involved in translation (and is also likely part of an operon), specific transcription factors only affect specific genes and not a particular issue in prokaryotes.
CM14	B	cancer is uncontrolled cell reproduction - reducing regulation of a related gene may cause cancer
CM15	D	RNA polII is responsible for mRNA production
CM16	E	A-C could all account for this transcription but lack of gene function
CM17	D	A missing charged tRNA would stop the extesnion of a polypeptide chain
CM18	B	Turner syndrome is the only monosomic condition that results in a living Human
CM19	C	A 0.0 is a 0% chance of being a random match

CM20	C	Only C and D are H-W assumptions; mutation is environmental and migration has changed (planes, trains and automobiles)
CM21	C	EST sequenciug provides a fast look at the transcribed genes
CM22	C	A/T content and G/C content are exactly related to each other; G/C content more common measure of strand
CM23	D	60% / 2 = 30%
CM24	B	In mitosis, the two resulting cells are equal diploid cells
CM25	C	Proposing a testable hypothesis is the next step
CM26	E	The central dogma is the core concept that covers replication of a cell
CM27	B	The start codon is ATG and is for methionine, the ATT (AUU) encodes Isoleucine (I), etc. the T's in the sequence must be converted to U's as RNA **CG ATG AUU CCU CAU UGU….**
CM28	A	The start codon is ATG and is for methionine, the TTC (UUC) encodes Phenylalnine (F), etc. the T's in the sequence must be converted to U's as RNA **CG ATG UUC CUC AUU GUC….**
CM29	A	Simply change the U's in the mRNA sequence to T's.
CM30	A, C, E, F, H are all H-W assumptions for equilibrium	
CM31	C	A, B, D are not valid factors; C would support the findings, but would likely not be much of a breakthrough.
CM32	B	complementary DNA (cDNA) is created from mRNA using reverse transcriptase
CM33	C	Alternative (exon) splicing allows the creation of multiple polypeptides from one gene.
CM34	C	Cysitc fibrosis is a specific, practical problem
CM35	A,B,D	Basic research advances our understanding of a subject, phenomenon or basic law of nature.
CM36	E	All are peer review - even if you are not discussing it, you are *always* performing peer review.
CM37	B	Peer review - this problem indicates that their controlled experiment was not well planned
CM38	E	All; but why C? An important first step is to identify who has the disease, where they live and to create an affected sample group along with an unaffected control group; this is often geographically based.
CM39	D	
CM40	B,C,D	A) a lot of international research is printed in English, so the language of the paper is likely not a factor B) The conclusions of the paper are not changed based on the language it it written in C and D) both C and D are valid questions and could be an interesting project.
CM41	C	
CM42	E	
CM43	A	
CM44	D	
CM45	D	
CM46	E	
CM47	E	
CM48	B	Introns are removed from mRNA before mRNA is exported from the nucleus
CM49	C	There are always one fewer introns than exons
CM50	D	There are always one fewer introns than exons
CM51	A	All mice died or were killed
CM52	A	All mice died or were killed
CM53	D	Only the removal of DNA from the heat-killed mixture led to living mice with no type IIIS bacteria.
CM54	D	
CM55	C	
CM56	D	
CM57	B	
CM58	B	
CM60	B	
CM59	A	
CM61	C	
CM62	D	
CM63	A	Only mRNA will be translated; rRNA and tRNA are functional molecules once they are transcribed
CM64	B	Only rRNA is used in translation; microRNA and siRNA regulate (remove mRNAs).
CM65	E	Only tRNA is used in translation; microRNA and siRNA regulate (remove mRNAs).
CM66	A	
CM67	B	
CM68	C	The higher the G/C content, the higher the melting Tm
CM69	A	Although typically stated as G/C content, the A/T content also can predict the melting temperature Tm of a strand of DNA (the higher the A/T content, the lower the temperature required)
CM70	E	
CM71	A	RNA polymerase is used for transcription of DNA into RNA
CM72	B	tRNA is used for translation of RNA into polypeptides
CM73	C	

CM74 B
CM75 B
CM76 C
CM77 B
CM78 A
CM78 A
CM79 D
CM80 A
CM81 B
CM82 C
CM83 B
CM84 E
CM85 A   Paralogous genes are in the same organism; non-coding DNA is essentially random; rRNA sequences are highly conserved due to the importance in an organism - not likely to have significant differences.
CM86 B   Overlapping error bars indicate that there are not enough readings to separate the two data points and that they *may* be statisitcally equal to each other.
CM87 B
CM88 D
CM89 C
CM90 A
CM91 D
CM92 A
CM93 A
CM94 B
CM95 E
CM96 A   ITS stands for internally transcribed spacer - although transcribed, the spacer must be sequenced to be of use in identification
CM97 D   This is about 1 in 1 million random chance (4^{10}) vs   (20^3) or 1 in 8,000 for C
CM98 C   This is about 1 in 8,000 (20^3) vs 1 in 4,000 (4^6) random chance for D
CM99 A   Between A and B, the RNA is a transcribed sequence compared against a transcribed sequence; Thus the random DNA of A is most likely to be random.
CM100 E   At first, this seems tough - just remember that for every five base pairs of DNA, you add three zeros; Thus at 20 base pairs, the chance of a random match is 000, 000, 000, 000 or 1,000,000,000,000 or 1 in one trillion.

CD Seq (CS)

CS1   5' - GCUCAUG - 3'
CS2   5' - TACGAGT - 3'
CS3   5' - UAGGUGU - 3'
CS4   5' - GAAGCGA - 3'
CS5   3' - AGCAGCA - 5'
CS6   5' - UACCAAU - 3'
CS7   5' - GAACGAT - 3'
CS8   3' - ACGTTAG - 5'
CS9   5' - UUGCAUC - 3'
CS10   3' - AGTATCG - 5'
CS11   3' - CGGAGCT - 5'
CS12   5' - TCTAGCG - 3'
CS13   5' - CGAUACC - 3'
CS14   3' - AAGCGTA - 5'
CS15   5' - UAAGUAC - 3'
CS16   3' - AGTGACG - 5'
CS17   5' - MT - 3'
CS18   5' - MSA - 3'
CS19   5' - MRL - 3'
CS20   5' - MCS - 3'

Central Dogma Long Answer (CLA)

CLA1   Stop codons in Plus 1, Plus 3, Minus 5 and Minus 6; no stop codon in Plus 2 or Minus 4 leaving these as open reading frames (a start codon is NOT required)

CLA2   RNA polymerase, DNA polymerase, DNA, Helicase, single-stranded binding proteins, topoisomerase, DNA ligase, RNA primer, DNA primer, free nucleotides, etc

CLA3   rRNA, tRNA, microRNA, siRNA, mRNA, RISC, amino acids, polypeptides, etc.

CLA4   They want to identify the SNP that is linked to breast cancer susceptibility in the FGFR2 gene and to propose a biological reason for the susceptibility

CLA5   That the eight strongly linked SNPs within the second intron can be identified as causative for breast cancer susceptibility by looking at FGFR2 expression in cell lines containing these SNPs (minor) vs cell lines without these SNPs (common)

CLA6   Using protein-DNA interactions to identify the most likely to alter affinity for transcription factors Oct-1/Runx2 and C/EBPb, they then measure expression within cell lines specifically containing these factors.

CLA7   (must have the full manuscript) The expression profiles of 13 cell lines of minor homozygotes (with both alleles containing the SNPs), 30 heterozygotes (one common, no SNP allele and one minor 8 SNP allele) and 20 common, no SNP allele cell lines.

CLA8   Prokaryotes have a single origin of replication acting on a circular genome; Eukaryotes have multiple origins of replication acting on multiple, linear chromosomes

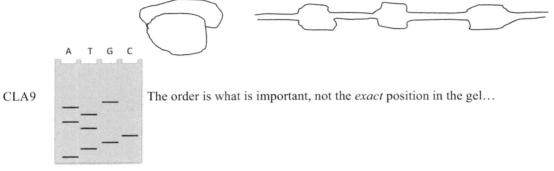

CLA9   The order is what is important, not the *exact* position in the gel…

CLA10   This is basic math with 4 to the sixth power; 4; 16; 64; 256; 1024; 4096; The odds are 1 in 4096 or 1/4096.

CLA11   This is basic math with 4 to the fourth power; 4; 16; 64; 256; The odds are 1 in 256 or 1/256.

CLA12   1) Proline will be inserted into the serine position of polypeptides, about 50% of the time (serine tRNA is still available). 2) The organism will likely die in short order, because…. 3) Any Proline codon in the mRNA will act as a stop codon.

CLA13   This is basic math with 20 to the fourth power; 20; 400; 8,000; 160,000; The odds are 1 in 160,000 or 1/160,000.

CLA14   To find out how much of blinding retinopathy is caused by changes in CRX gene expression.

CLA15   That phenotypic differences in blinding retinopathy can be correlated with the amount of CRX RNA present in mouse models with known genetic mutations in the CRX gene

CLA16   Collect CRX and rod and cone transcript data (RNA) from the mouse models and compare with disease severity

CLA17   Transcript abundance and phenotype variation

CLA18   That minor changes in transcript level can result in "huge" phenotypic variation and that the molecular mechanisms involved have been more described for future study.

Transmission Genetics True/False (TTF)

TTF1   A

TTF2   A

TTF3   A

TTF4   B   son must be a carrier due to affected father

TTF5   A

TTF6   A

TTF7   B   mother must be a carrier to have affected son

TTF8   A

TTF9   A

TTF10 B   No carriers in dominant traits, mother indicated as a carrier

TTF11 B   son must be a carrier due to affected father

TTF12 B   homozygous 216/216 daughter not possible

TTF13 B   Pedigree is made from SSR molecular markers

TTF14 B   Pedigree is made from SNP molecular markers

TTF15 B   "G" allele in daughter cannot be inherited from either parent

TTF16 A
TTF17 A
TTF18 A
TTF19 B   Phenotype-based inheritance shown, not molecular marker-based
TTF20 B   Father cannot pass on mitochondrial disease
TTF21 T
TTF22 F   No affected parent for III-6
TTF23 F   II-3 and III-3 would be affected
TTF24 F   I-1 would have to be affected and is required to pass affected allele to II-3
TTF25 T
TTF26 F   All males in generation III should be affected to some degree.
TTF27 F   All children of II-1 and II-2 will be affected; The children of two individuals affected by an autosomal recessive disease will all be affected
TTF28 T
TTF29 T   Although II-1 cannot inherit the trait from I-2, they can still have the trait (although it is unlikely)
TTF30 F   All children of II-2 should be affected to a degree; III-6 does not have an affected mother and cannot inherit from father II-3.

Transmission Genetics - Multiple Choice (TM)

TM1   E   Anticipation is indicated when a disease is presented earlier in each generation of a family
TM2   E   Heterosis is the condition where an offspring has a trait greater than either parent.
TM3   D
TM4   C   Autosomal recessive requires alleles from both parents, Male to female gen I to II precludes mitochondrial, X-linked recessive requires alleles from both parents for affected females
TM5   E   All of the F1 seed will be smooth - the smooth trait is dominant (note the capital "S")
TM6   E   All of the wrinkled seed are homozygous recessive
TM7   B   Because the parents of the victim are homozygous, they must 120/120 and 125/125; only suspect 6 has the required alleles to be a sibling.
TM8   B
TM9   B, C   Both of these have an (the same) affected parent.
TM10   C   The ratio gets closer to 3:1 as more data is taken
TM11   E   Band size represents the base pairs between two points in DNA; This is a phenotype
TM12   D
TM13   A   Our future is doomed if you picked plug-in....
TM14   C
TM15   E
TM16   A
TM17   A
TM18   D   A test cross is easily done by several methods that are less tedious than crossing two individuals
TM19   D   Heterozygote individuals are carriers, not affected
TM20   A   The are no unaffected individuals in dominant diseases
TM21   E
TM22   C
TM23   D
TM24   D
TM25   B
TM26   B   Not "D"; female heterozygotes are carriers
TM27   C
TM28   D   The most common disorder in Humans is color-blindness
TM29   A
TM30   C
TM31   D
TM32 A, B, D
TM33   E   All of these can introduce Cis (the same) genes into an organism
TM34   B,D   Lentivrus are used for animals; Backcrossing requires cross-able organisms
TM35   C   Because this is a Transgenic modification into an animal genome, crossing and gene-gun manipulation are not possible
TM36   B
TM37   E   SSN is not a marker type

TM38	A	
TM39	A	An SSR or microsatellite marker is a size-based marker that MUST be detected using electrophoresis
TM40	B	
TM41	E	"15/18" means that the tested alleles have 15 repeats in one and 18 repeats in the other
TM42	C	
TM43	A	
TM44	B	
TM45	C	
TM46	D	
TM47	E	
TM48	A	
TM49	B	
TM50	B	
TM51	D	
TM52	C	
TM53	B	
TM54	D	
TM55	E	
TM56	A	1 standard deviation is 68% of the population. This leaves 32% remaining; half of these are taller, while half are shorter.
TM57	B	The definition of a lethal allele is that homozygous recessive progeny does not survive
TM58	E	
TM59	A	organelles are randomly segregated during mitosis into each daughter cell, meaning that each subsequent cell line is based on the organelles received during the previous mitosis events.
TM60-64		II-4, II-7, II-8, III-4, III-8 MUST be carriers
TM60	C	
TM61	D	
TM62	A	
TM63	B	II-8 carrier, II-9 unaffected; Males cannot be carriers and only half of the daughters will inherit the allele from their mother
TM64	C	All male progeny would be affected, all female progeny would be carriers
TM65-TM70		Given genotypes: I-1 150/160; II-4 130/170; II-9 120/130; III-2 130/160; III-4 160/160; III-5 150/170; III-7 120/130; III-12 120/170; Derived Genotypes II-3 120/150, II-8 170, II-2 160/- II-1 130/160, I-2 120/170
TM65	D	
TM66	C	
TM67	D	
TM68	A	
TM69	B	
TM70	E	None are possible combinations of I-1 and I-2
TM71	D	
TM72	B	
TM73	C	
TM74	A	
TM75	B	
TM76	A	
TM77	E	
TM78	B	
TM79	E	
TM80	C	All of the Tt plants are taller - this is a hybrid vigor/heterosis question
TM81	C	both TT and tt are shorter, thus 50% - this is a hybrid vigor/heterosis question
TM82	B	the tt progeny - this is a hybrid vigor/heterosis question
TM83	C	
TM84	B	
TM85	B	
TM86	B	Only half of the daughters will be carriers, all sons inheriting the allele will be affected
TM87	B	Half of the sons will likely inherit the disease and be affected.
TM88	C	Half of the daughters and half of the sons will not inherit the allele from their mother.
TM89	C	½ x ½ x ½ = 1/8
TM90	E	¼ x ½ x ¼ = 1/32
TM91	D	¼ x ½ x ½ = 1/16
TM92	A	

TM93	B	
TM94	B	
TM95	E	
TM96	A	
TM97	B	
TM98	E	This test cross yields unexpected results
TM99	B	Even though the number of replications is low, it is clear that the unknown is heterozygous
TM100	D	The number of progeny is too low to make a determination between A or B; The random chance of a B/b individual having four B/b children is ½ x ½ x ½ x ½ = 1/16 or about 6%.

Transmission Genetics Pedigrees (TP)

TP1   Parents of II-5 (I-1 and I-2); Parents of III-2 and III-4 (II-1 and II-4) each received copy from I-1 or I-2.

TP2   50%

TP3   First, determine who MUST be a carrier; In this case, III-3 and III-4 are obvious, but so are II-2 and II-5. *Test them? sure, why not*...Second, who would need to know? IV-1, III-1, III-2 and III-5 *should be tested* because they are still young enough to potentially have children. Testing generation II might be informative, but they are likely in their 40s t o 50s, so are unlikely to have more children.

TP4   Either by directly sequencing any samples that may have been preserved, testing either side of their extended families descendents. In the end it would not be a useful endeavor , since it would not change the carrier or disease status of the current generations.

TP5   III-1; The proband is the person who brings the family under study and since tIII-1 is the only one showing symptoms of the disease, the would be the proband

TP6   II-1 is II-2s first husband and is relevant due to their child; II-3 is II-2s second husband, who is likewise relevant due to their two children

TP7   II-1 and II-2 MUST be carriers

TP8   Either I-1 or I-2; possibly II-4 or II-6; Possibly children of II-4, III-4, III-5, III-6.

TP9   V-1, V-3, V-4, V-5, V-6, III-3, III-4, II-1, II-4

TP10   IV-1, III-1, III-2, III-6, II-3; I-1 or I-2 is a carrier

TP11   Generation V is already married; must be at least 20 years old, add 20 years minimum for each generation; at latest 1920 but more likely before 1900.

TP9   V-1, V-3, V-4, V-5, V-6, III-3, III-4, II-1, II-4

TP10   IV-1, III-1, III-2, III-6, II-3; I-1 or I-2 is a carrier

TP11   Generation V is already married; must be at least 20 years old, add 20 years minimum for each generation; at latest 1920 but more likely before 1900.

TP12   Daughters of II-2 (III-1 and III-2) are carriers; Daughter of II-4 (III-4) is a carrier; Mother of II-2 and II-4 (I-2) is a carrier

TP13   Daughters of II-2 and II-3 are carriers (III-1 and III-3)

TP14   V-5 MIGHT be a carrier; III-5 is a carrier

TP15   Sons of affected I-2 are affected (II-2, II-3, II-5, II-6); III-4 might be affected (if II-4 is affected)

TP16   II-2 gives to III-1, III-2 and III-3; I-2 gives to II-1, II-2, II-5; II-5 transmits to III-4 and III-5

TP17   II-1 passes to III-1; either II-5 or II-6 as a parent of III-5; If II-5 is affected, I-2 must also be affected

TP18   Derive I-1 16/27 from II-2 and II-6; Add 16 to II-1 from III-1 – because II-2 cannot be 27/16 (must get one copy from each parent); Now add 17 to II-2 from III-2; Derive 19/24 for II-5 by using only those sizes that are not in the parents of II-4. This leaves 27/31 for II-4 derived from remaining III-3 and III-4 children

TP19   Derive III-2, III-3, III-4 as 310 from homozygous parent II-4; Derive II-1, II-3 and II-5 as 330 from homozygous parent I-2; Derive II-1 325 from child III-1, then derive I-1 325 from II-1; Derive II-3 315 from child III-4, then derive I-1 315 from II-3; Derive II-6 320 from child III-5 (Parents I-1 and I-2 do not have 320, must come from II-6).

TP20   Derive II-2 and II-3 C from III-4; Add C to II-3 (known homozygous), then add C to III-3 from II-3; Derive II-1 AT from III-1 and III-2 (these alleles cannot be from II-2); Derive II-5 C from III-6; II-2 and II-5 only share a C, so this must be the homozygous allele - CC to I-1, A to I-2

Transmission Genetics Long Answer/Calculation

TLA1-3 Identify the father by using a highlighter or colored pencil; the father is the only one who could have provided one of the alleles for every marker in the daughter.

TLA1   Alleles unique to **father 1** in child 1 are D7S820 216, VWA160, etc…

TLA2   Alleles unique to **father 3** in child 2 are TPOX 227, D3S1358 112, etc…

TLA3   Alleles unique to **father 1** in child 3 are TPOX 220, FGA 300, etc…

TLA4-6 First, cricle the alleles from father 1 in children 1 and 3. Then circle the alleles from father 3 in child 2. You are simply selecting alleles that had to come from the father - in other words, for TPOX in child 1 the alleles are 216 and 220, but their father only has 220 and 220 - thus the 220 allele must come from father 1. Circle all alleles from each father in this manner - what is left is what must have come from the mother. In the case of FGA, CSF1PO, D7S820 and TH01, it is unclear as to whether the mother is homozygous for the allele indicated or if her second allele was simply not transmitted to any of her three children.

TLA4 216/237

TLA5 136/165

TLA6 122/160

TLA7 Between the three children there are six alleles at each molecular marker locus, but only four alleles between the parents. If there are five unique alleles at any locus, there must be a second father. In the example below the five parental alleles for D3S1358 indicate a second father. It gets even easier with more than three children - there is still a four allele limit....

example:

Marker	Child 1	Child 2	Child 3	Parental alleles
TPOX	216/220	227/237	220/237	216, 220 227, 237
D3S1358	99/147	99/112	106/134	99, 147, 112, 106, 134

TLA8 II-3/II-4

TLA9 II-8/II-9

TLA10 III-6/III-7

TLA11 II-4

Population Genetics True/False (PTF)

PTF1 T
PTF2 F
PTF3 F
PTF4 T
PTF5 F
PTF6 T
PTF7 T
PTF8 F
PTF9 T
PTF10 T
PTF11 T
PTF12 T
PTF13 F
PTF14 T
PTF15 F
PTF16 T
PTF17 F
PTF18 T
PTF19 T
PTF20 F
PTF21 F
PTF22 F
PTF23 T
PTF24 F
PTF25 T
PTF26 F
PTF27 T
PTF28 T
PTF29 T
PTF30 F

Population Genetics Multiple Choice (PM)

PM1 E Environmental factors are not inherited
PM2 A, C, D survival of the fittest and the central dogma are not H-W assumptions
PM3 D The progeny inherited a dominant mutation - it is immediately evident

PM4	D	Somatic cells are not part of gamete production and new mutations cannot be transmitted to the next generation
PM5	E	
PM6	D	start with square root of affected; q = .4, p = .6; $p^2+2pq + q^2$; $.6^2 + 2(.6)(.4) + .4^2$ = 36 unaffected homozygous + 48 heterozygous carriers + 16 affected
PM7	A	start with square root of affected; q = .6, p = .4; $p^2+2pq + q^2$; $.4^2 + 2(.4)(.6) + .6^2$ = 16 unaffected homozygous + 48 heterozygous carriers + 36 affected
PM8	C	
PM9	E	
PM10	A	
PM11	C	The greatest variation is due to the smallest population size
PM12	A	The sequence in A is mRNA (note the U's); a TATATA repeat would result in a UAUAUAUA sequence in mRNA
PM13	D	Each new event reduces the genetic polymorphism from the source population
PM14	A,C,D	
PM15	C	"p" indicates polypeptide. "Thr" indicates the amino acid threonine.
PM16	B,E	
PM17	A, B, C	
PM18	D	
PM19	C;	a 1 bp deletion causes a frameshift in a gene encoding region
PM20	A or D are acceptable answers;	
PM21	B;	Frameshift will lead to very early termination
PM22	E;	B and C are not valid mutation notations (B "c" denotes sequence but shows amino acid; C "p" denotes polypeptide but shows DNA)
PM23	A	
PM24	D	
PM25	C	Exons often experience selection against mutations that harm the function of the gene
PM26	A	
PM27	A	Wild types are the most prevalent in a specific population
PM28	D	divide the numbers given by ten to make the calculation easier….100 people, 4 affected; q=.2, p = 0.8
PM29	C	divide the numbers given by ten to make the calculation easier….100 people, 4 affected; q=0.2, p=0.8.
PM30	D	….100 people, 4 affected; q=.2; p = 0.8
PM31	A	…….20 people, 5 affected; q=.5; p = 0.5; (0.5 x 0.5 = 25% are affected, 50% heterozygous and 25% homozygous unaffected) This is a Punnett square.
PM32	B;	….20 people, 5 affected; q=.5; p = 0.5; (0.5 x 0.5 = 25% are affected, 50% heterozygous and 25% homozygous unaffected) This is a Punnett square.
PM33	E	
PM34	D	Nine healthy children as carriers represents .25 to the ninth power or ¼ x ¼ x ¼ nine times or ~1/250.000 chance of happening with two carrier parents
PM35	D	Although an autosomal recessive disease is possible, since they are unrelated, disjunction is most likely cause
PM36	B	Relatedness of the parents means the most likely explanation is a shared autosomal recessive carrier condition
PM37	C	An autosomal dominant disease would explain this inheritance. The more severe symptom child is likely homozygous for the disease allele.
PM38	A	
PM39	D	
PM40	D	
PM41	E	
PM42	D	Because the mutation is spontaneous, it is unlikely a cousin would also have it (B); The new carrier is also unlikely to encounter another individual that has the same mutation or potential disease (c)
PM43	A	A chromosome addition results in Patau, Edwards or Down syndromes
PM44	A	Males cannot be carriers of X-linked diseases; Progeny with the de-novo (new) mutation will have the disease
PM45	C	
PM46	E	
PM47	A	
PM48	C	
PM49	C	complementary sequence to mutation
PM50	E	complementary sequence to mutation
PM51	D	Only serial founding events cause reduction of polymorphism in the initial population and the group migrating from the initial population. (bottleneck affects only one population)
PM52	B	Bottleneck events occur to a single population and reduce their diversity
PM53	C,D	

PM54 E
PM55 E   Autosomal recessive means that you have two diesease alleles - all children will be at least carriers.
PM56 B   Males can have unaffected sons or can use (B) to have non-carrier daughters
PM57 E   Affected Females must pass on the allele to all children (E)
PM58 C
PM59 D
PM60 A
PM61 C

Population Genetics Allele Calculations (PA)

PA1   36   Start with square root of affected; $q = .4$ thus $p = .6$;
$p^2+2pq + q^2$; $.6^2 + 2(.6)(.4) + .4^2 = 36$ homozygous unaffected + 48 heterozygous carriers + 16 affected

PA2   48   Start with square root of affected; $q = .4$ thus $p = .6$;
$p^2+2pq + q^2$; $.6^2 + 2(.6)(.4) + .4^2 = 36$ homozygous unaffected + 48 heterozygous carriers + 16 affected

PA3   84   Start with square root of affected; $q = .4$ thus $p = .6$;
$p^2+2pq + q^2$; $.6^2 + 2(.6)(.4) + .4^2 = 36$ homozygous unaffected + 48 heterozygous carriers + 16 affected

PA4   64   Because this disease is dominant, the p^2 and $2pq$ represent *affected* people. First, find q, which is 1.0 - affected (36) which = .64; the square root of .64 is .8 and this is q (and p is .2). Now solve the equation; $p^2+2pq + q^2$; $.2^2 + 2(.2)(.8) + .8^2 = 4$ homozygous affected + 32 heterozygous affected + 64 homozygous unaffected

PA5   4   Because this disease is dominant, the p^2 and $2pq$ represent *affected* people. First, find q, which is 1.0 - affected (36) which = .64; the square root of .64 is .8 and this is q (and p is .2). Now solve the equation; $p^2+2pq + q^2$; $.2^2 + 2(.2)(.8) + .8^2 = 4$ homozygous affected + 32 heterozygous affected + 64 homozygous unaffected

PA6   32   Because this disease is dominant, the p^2 and $2pq$ represent *affected* people. First, find q, which is 1.0 - affected (36) which = .64; the square root of .64 is .8 and this is q (and p is .2). Now solve the equation; $p^2+2pq + q^2$; $.2^2 + 2(.2)(.8) + .8^2 = 4$ homozygous affected + 32 heterozygous affected + 64 homozygous unaffected

PA7   9   Start with square root of affected; $q = .3$ thus $p = .7$; $p^2+2pq + q^2$; $.7^2 + 2(.7)(.3) + .3^2 = $ 49 homozygous unaffected + 42 heterozygous carriers + 9 homozygous affected

PA8   42   Start with square root of affected; $q = .3$ thus $p = .7$; $p^2+2pq + q^2$; $.7^2 + 2(.7)(.3) + .3^2 = $ 49 homozygous unaffected + 42 heterozygous carriers + 9 homozygous affected

PA9   49   Start with square root of affected; $q = .3$ thus $p = .7$; $p^2+2pq + q^2$; $.7^2 + 2(.7)(.3) + .3^2 = $ 49 homozygous unaffected + 42 heterozygous carriers + 9 homozygous affected

PA10   1   Start with square root of affected; $q = .1$ thus $p = .9$; $p^2+2pq + q^2$; $.9^2 + 2(.9)(.1) + .1^2 = $ 81 homozygous unaffected + 18 heterozygous carriers + 1 homozygous affected

PA11   81   Start with square root of affected; $q = .1$ thus $p = .9$; $p^2+2pq + q^2$; $.9^2 + 2(.9)(.1) + .1^2 = $ 81 homozygous unaffected + 18 heterozygous carriers + 1 homozygous affected

PA12   18   Start with square root of affected; $q = .1$ thus $p = .9$; $p^2+2pq + q^2$; $.9^2 + 2(.9)(.1) + .1^2 = $ 81 homozygous unaffected + 18 heterozygous carriers + 1 homozygous affected

PA13   13   Start with square root of affected; $q = 0.005$ or 0.07) thus $p = .93$; $p^2+2pq + q^2$; $.93^2 + 2(.93)(.07) + .07^2 = $ 86.5 homozygous unaffected + 13 heterozygous carriers + 0.5 homozygous affected

PA14   86.5   Start with square root of affected; $q = 0.005$ or 0.07) thus $p = .93$; $p^2+2pq + q^2$; $.93^2 + 2(.93)(.07) + .07^2 = $ 86.5 homozygous unaffected + 13 heterozygous carriers + 0.5 homozygous affected

PA15   99.5   Start with square root of affected; $q = 0.005$ or 0.07) thus $p = .93$; $p^2+2pq + q^2$; $.93^2 + 2(.93)(.07) + .07^2 = $ 86.5 homozygous unaffected + 13 heterozygous carriers + 0.5 homozygous affected

PA16   96.38%   Start with the square root of affected; $(q = \sqrt{0.000333}$ or 0.01825) thus $p = .98175$;
$p^2+2pq + q^2$; $.98175^2 + 2(0.98175)(0.01825) + 0.01825^2 = $
96.38% homozygous unaffected + 3.58% heterozygous carriers + 0.000333% homozygous affected

PA17   3.58%   Start with the square root of affected; $(q = \sqrt{0.000333}$ or 0.01825) thus $p = .98175$;
$p^2+2pq + q^2$; $.98175^2 + 2(0.98175)(0.01825) + 0.01825^2 = $
96.38% homozygous unaffected + 3.58% heterozygous carriers + 0.000333% homozygous affected

PA18   99.97%   Start with the square root of affected; $(q = \sqrt{0.000333}$ or 0.01825) thus $p = .98175$;
$p^2+2pq + q^2$; $0.98175^2 + 2(0.98175)(0.01825) + 0.01825^2 = $
96.38% homozygous unaffected + 3.58% heterozygous carriers + 0.000333% homozygous affected

Population Genetics Long Answer (PLA)

There are many possible answers - the following is literally my opinion and should NOT be used as the sole grading source.

PLA1   Although male fertility would be reduced, no change in the male:female ratio would occur - the number of males able to have children would be reduced.

PLA2   Since there is apparently little to no effect on litter sizes, this is a tough one. The difficulty in answering this question lies in the fact that as part of the litter, a carrier female would have 50% affected male offspring, essentially unable to sire the next generation. Perhaps an increased female mating drive might compensate.

PLA3   The hypothesis is that a Dmc1 defective allele mouse population will produce the same number of progeny after "x" generations (you could use time as well). Providing consistent habitats and resources to both populations, you would allow the two populations to develop for the necessary generations/time, then you would count the number of progeny in each group. Perhaps creating data such as pedigree trees and Dmc1 allele status from each mouse. If the same number of individuals were in each group at the end of the study, you might change your hypothesis to a behavioural study, attempting to discover if a social cue was responsible.

PLA4   It will likely decrease random mating - since monogamous relationships reduce the mating choice for both individuals.

PLA5   Just a guess here - maybe those pre-disposed to EPM will migrate away from the society, leaving those that operate within this population to potentially lead more monogamous lives - and produce a less diverse populaion.

PLA6   Possibly reduce it - if monogamy is forced in a population, then unreproductive pairs will likely produce fewer offspring.

PLA7   Oh my. The resource is the woman, who is partitioning the ability to produce offspring to more than one mate.

PLA8   Random Mating: Once homozygous recessive individuals begin to use the new resource (milk from domestic animals) they will be more reproductively successful, eventually leading to a preponderance of persistent lactose tolerance in the population

PLA9   Migration: Because migration was limited during most of this time frame, those who were able to utilize dairy products were more likely to concentrate in the same region, increasing the prevalence of the allele. This is also why the allele is so common in Europe, but less common in Africa and Asia.

PLA10   Genetic Drift: At least initially, the populations who domesticated animals were small in number. Therefore the allele would have been more easily incorporated into later generations

PLA11   Association mapping - it even says this in the results section

PLA12   This is a bit tougher - The SNPs would be in A T G or C format and would likely reflect the % homozygousity and heterozygousity for each population tested. The disease data would be population-wide and based on specific regions, while the environmental variables may be in the form of average temp, precipitation, etc. This would lead to an effort to associate these alleles with the environmental conditions

PLA13   Migration out of Africa is actually illustrated in Figure 14.1, which shows that migration occurred from the African continent about 100,000 years ago, then eventually spread throughout the world.

PLA14   The serial founder effect is a way of describing how populations changed during human migration. When a small number of individuals comprise the total population of a region, eventually the traits within that small group will become prevalent. This is why people of European and Asian descent are phenotypically different. The differences between populations become even more pronounced when a small founding population is again formed from a population that was itself formed by a small group of individuals.

PLA15   This could be both. The declining rates of risk alleles from diabetes would seem to indicate that the alleles were more concentrated in the African population, which then was reduced as smaller populations migrated. Likewise, an argument could be made that as separate founder populations continued migrating, the diabetes allele was selected against

Lab Questions (LAB)

LAB1   Blowout, eject aspirate and dispense (BEAD)

LAB2   Water, DNA polymerase, buffer, free nucleotides, DNA template, primers, $MgCl_2$

LAB3   873 ul

LAB4   3 ul

LAB5   The samples would evaporate due to the heated lid being below 100° C

LAB6   P2 only has one amplification band

LAB7   This is not the disease allele since it segregates with all subjects and is not homozygous in the affected individuals

LAB8   This is a dominant disease, since it requires only the 500 bp allele to produce the disease

LAB9   Neither child is a carrier - there are no carriers in dominant diseases

LAB10   P1 (two alleles corresponds to 2 X chromosomes)

LAB11   This is the disease allele since it segregates with all affected subjects

LAB12   This is a recessive disease, since the two females P1 and C2 do not have the disease, but the two males P2 and C1, both males, are hemizygous for the disease.

LAB13   C2 is a carrier

LAB14   Father passed his 900 bp and mother passed her 500 bp.

LAB15   B

LAB16   E   This sequence has a 60% G/C content (the highest of all possible answers)

LAB17   C   This sequence has a 30% G/C content (the lowest of all possible answers)

LAB18   D   This has a 6bp recognition site, or about once every 4,000 bp of random DNA

LAB19   A   This has a 4bp recognition site, or about once every 250 bp of random DNA

LAB20 B   One amino acid is encoded by each codon
LAB21 A   One amino acid is encoded by each codon, each codon is 3 bp 3 x 930 = 2,790
LAB22 C   One amino acid is encoded by each codon
LAB23 B   ITS database is used extensivley to identify bacterial unknowns
LAB24 C
LAB25 A   No organism type is specified
LAB26 A
LAB27 C
LAB28 A
LAB29 B
LAB30 E
LAB31 D
LAB32 C   Use the rule of 3 000s for every 5 base pairs
LAB33 D   Use the rule of 3 000s for every 5 base pairs
LAB34 E   Use the rule of 3 000s for every 5 base pairs
LAB35 D   equals 2.15 ml or 0.00215 L; E is a distance..
LAB36 C   2.1 mg = 2.1 ul of water, barely the size of a pin head.
LAB37 Institution specific
LAB38 Institution specific
LAB39 Institution specific
LAB40 Institution specific
LAB41 F
LAB42 F; DNA is not consumed in the PCR reaction
LAB43 F; 100o C
LAB44 T
LAB45 T
LAB46 T
LAB47 T
LAB48 T
LAB49 F
LAB50 F

Central Dogma Exam

1 ____ The following sequences are possible (True) or not possible (False)
5' - UCGAUCAG - 3' mRNA
3' - TCGATCAG - 5' coding DNA
5' - AGCTAGTC - 3' template DNA

2 ____ In DNA gel electrophoresis, samples run towards negative/red (True/False)

3 ____ Griffith discovered that the transforming material was RNA (True/False)

4 ____ Watson and Crick discovered that DNA was replicated in a conservative manner (True/False)

5 ____ Prokaryote RNA has multiple origins of replication (True/False)

6 ____ Housekeeping genes are always expressed (True/False)

7 ____ Housekeeping genes are differentially expressed (True/False)

8 ____ Alternative splicing means that an exon can be removed from a transcript (True/False)

9 ____ RNA polymerase III is required for mRNA synthesis (True/False)

10 ____ RNA polymerase II is required for tRNA synthesis (True/False)

11 ____ There are several exceptions to the codons used for polypeptide synthesis (True/False)

12 ____ A charged mRNA brings an amino acid in to a ribosome for incorporation into a polypeptide (True/False)

13 ____ The process that utilizes DNA polymerase is:
A   mitosis   D   meiosis II
B   transcription   E   All of the above
C   Ribosomal Polymerase Reaction

14 ____ You need this molecule to make microRNA
A   DNA polymerase   D   tRNA
B   DNA Template   E   mRNA
C   Ribosomes

15 ____ RNA polymerase is not required for which of the following
A   mRNA   D   RNAse
B   tRNA   E   rRNA
C   microRNA

16 ____ The process associated with RNA polymerase is:
A   mitosis   D   meiosis II
B   transcription   E   All of the above
C   translation

17 ____ Which of the following is needed to perform PCR (may be more than one)?
A   Ribosome   D   Primers
B   DNA polymerase   E   Topoisomerase
C   RNA polymerase I

18 ____ Commonly used name for a PCR machine
A   DNA Doubler   D   Thermal Cycler
B   Mullis-Microwave   E   None of the above
C   Taq cycler

19 ____ Incorporation of amino acids into a growing polypeptide has stopped, which one of the following molecules is most likely lacking in the cell?
A microRNA   D charged tRNA
B ribosome   E rRNA
C polysome

20 ____ You notice a missing chromosome in a patients karyotype - which of these conditions is caused by monosomy?
A Patau Syndrome   D Parkinsons Disease
B Turner Syndrome   E All of the above are possible
C Huntingtons Disease

21 ____ Which of the following represents the best possible (not likely to be random) "e" value from a BLAST result?
A 0.15   D 7e-150
B 6.1   E 6e-24
C 0.0

22 ____ The temperature required to separate two complementary strands of the same DNA molecule is affected by which of the following factors?
A The direction of the strand   D The availability of DNA helicase
B The A/C content of the strand   E The availability of DNA Polymerase
C The A/T content of the strand

23 ____ In a diploid cell, mitosis leads to:
A Four haploid gametes   D Four daughter cells
B Two daughter cells   E Two haploid gametes
C One diploid daughter cell and two haploid gametes

24 ____ Which of the following represent applied research?
A Describing the structure of kinetochores
B Identifying the molecules involved in transcription
C Finding the gene responsible for cystic fibrosis
D Identifying the molecules involved in translation
E None of the above

25 ____ A mutation is important for which of the following fields of Genetics?
A Transmission Genetics   D A-C are all mutation-based
B Population Genetics   E None of the above are affected by mutation
C The Central Dogma

26 ____ Which of the following carry out their functions in the cytoplasm?
A microRNA   D mRNA
B siRNA   E All carry out their functions in the cytoplasm
C tRNA

27 ____ Which of the following are not exported from the nucleus?
A microRNA   D mRNA
B Introns   E All are exported from the nucleus
C Exons

28 ____ You have a gene with 15 introns. How many exons are in this gene?
A 5   D 16
B 3   E Unable to determine
C 14

29 ____ In the Avery et al. experiments, removal of which molecule from the heat-killed mixture led to the isolation of type IIIS bacteria from dead mice?

A Polysaccharides   D All of the above

B Protein   E None of the above

C RNA

30 ____ The process in which each strand of DNA separates and each is used as a template to create a new double-stranded DNA molecule

A Semi-conservative replication   D Initiation

B Transcription   E None of the above

C Translation

31 ____ Which of the following molecules will be translated?

A mRNA   D siRNA

B rRNA   E tRNA

C microRNA

32 ____ The temperature required to separate two complementary strands of the same DNA molecule is affected by which of the following factors?

A The A/T content of the strand   D The availability of DNA helicase

B The direction of the strand   E The availability of DNA polymerase

C The G/T content of the strand

33 ____ Which of the following molecules is NOT required for DNA replication in a cell?

A RNA polymerase   D Single stranded binding proteins

B Topoisomerase   E all are required for DNA replication in a cell

C Helicase

34 ____ The part of a tRNA that holds an amino acid when "charged"

A Magnetic arm   D Holder-arm

B Anti-codon sequence   E None of the above

C Acceptor arm

35 ____ When a polypeptide, a coding sequence and an mRNA are all read in the same direction

A Complementary base pairing   D Transcription/translation stability

B Co-linearity of gene expression   E None of the above

C Polymerase gene order

36 ____ A group of cells that carry a mutation that causes unchecked cell growth but do not move from their initial tissue location.

A Malignant cancer cells   D Un-methylated cancer cells

B Benign cancer cells   E None of the above

C Methylated cancer cells

37 ____ A condition in which a *normal* number of chromosomes are present

A Euploid   D Aneuploid

B Diploid   E None of the above

C Haploid

38 ____ A mutation is located on chromosome 1q13.2. What does this mean?

A The mutation is on the small arm of chromosome 1

B The mutation is on the long arm of chromosome 1

C The mutation is in the first gene of chromosome q

D The mutation is in the 1st exon of the 13th gene on chromosome q

E None of the above

39 ____   It is 2015; you wish to identify a prokaryotes via ITS DNA. Which technology would you be able to use?
    A   Fluorescent Sanger sequencing   D   Transcriptomics
    B   Microsatellite diversity   E   All of the above
    C   Single nucleotide polymorphisms (SNPs)

40 ____   Which of the following is *least* likely to be random?
    A   Four DNA base pairs matching four DNA base pairs in another sample
    B   Four RNA base pairs matching four RNA base pairs in another sample
    C   Three amino acids matching three amino acids in another sample
    D   Ten DNA base pairs matching Ten DNA base pairs in another sample

41 ____   A common size for a polymerase chain reaction primer is 20 bp. How specific is this?
    A   About One in a million   D   About One in One Hundred Billion
    B   About One in One Hundred Million E   About one in a Trillion
    C   About One in a Billion

42   Derive the missing Template strand. Indicate the 5' and 3' ends of your sequence

mRNA   __' - U C G U C G U - __'

DNA Coding   __' - __ __ __ __ __ __ __ - __'

DNA Template   __' - __ __ __ __ __ __ __ - __'

43   Derive the missing Template strand. Indicate the 5' and 3' ends of your sequence

DNA Coding   __' - T G C A A T C - __'

DNA Template   __' - __ __ __ __ __ __ __ - __'

44   Derive the missing mRNA strand. Indicate the 5' and 3' ends of your sequence

mRNA   __' - __ __ __ __ __ __ __ - __'

DNA Coding   __' - __ __ __ __ __ __ __ - __'

DNA Template   __' - A A C G T A G - __'

45   Derive the missing mRNA strand. Indicate the 5' and 3' ends of your sequence

mRNA   __' - __ __ __ __ __ __ __ - __'

DNA Coding   __' - __ __ __ __ __ __ __ - __'

DNA Template   __' - G C T A T G G - __'

46   Derive the missing Template strand. Indicate the 5' and 3' ends of your sequence

mRNA   __' - U U C G C A U - __'

DNA Coding   __' - __ __ __ __ __ __ __ - __'

DNA Template   __' - __ __ __ __ __ __ __ - __'

47 List five central dogma molecules that carry out their function in the cytoplasm

48 Draw prokaryote and eukaryote replication forks. Identify what is different about the two different processes.

49 Calculate the odds (in fractions) of encountering the sequence 5' - ATACGA - 3' in a random fragment of DNA.

50 Calculate the odds (in fractions) of encountering the sequence 5' - PRNL - 3' in a random polypeptide

Transmission Genetics Exam

1 _____ You are treating a family that has Huntingtons disease. You obtain sequence from the HTT gene for each affected family member and notice that the younger members of the family are presenting the disease earlier than their older relatives. What repeat-based phenomenon could explain this?

  A   Mono-genic inheritance   D   An induced transcription factor
  B   Trisomy   E   Anticipation
  C   Defective (Recessive) allele

2 _____ You have a child. This child's fingers are longer than you or your spouse/other biological parents fingers. What is the likely reason?

  A   Heterosis   D   Smart chromosome Trisomy
  B   Incomplete dominance   E   None of the Above
  C   Massive Mendelian Inheritance

3 _____ Mendel crossed homozygous parents with smooth (SS) and wrinkled (ss) seed to make heterozygous smooth F1 seed. These F1 seed were then selfed. What is the chance that an F1 seed chosen at random will be wrinkled?

  A   75%   D   66%
  B   25%   E   0%
  C   33%

4 _____ Mendel crossed homozygous parents with smooth (SS) and wrinkled (ss) seed to make heterozygous smooth F1 seed. These F1 seed were then selfed. What is the chance that a wrinkled F2 seed will produce smooth seeds when selfed?

  A   75%   D   66%
  B   25%   E   0%
  C   33%

5 _____ More males are affected by a disease with this inheritance pattern

  A   Autosomal Dominant   D   Homozygous Lethal
  B   X-Linked Recessive   E   None of the above
  C   X-Linked Dominant

6 _____ Why did Mendel come closest to a 3:1 ratio with seed color (6022 yellow:2001 green; 3.01:1)?

  A   Yellow was dominant   D   Because seed color is easy to see
  B   Green had fewer seed   E   All of the above
  C   He had taken the most data with this trait

7 _____ Which of the following is NOT a phenotype?

  A   Flower color   D   Seed color
  B   Plant Height   E   All are phenotypes
  C   DNA Agarose electrophoresis band size

8 _____ A cross in which only one trait is analyzed

  A   monohybrid   D   Plug-in hybrid
  B   Di-hybrid   E   A Phillips cross
  C   single trait hybrid

9 _____ Mendel verified his plants were pure-line hybrids by....
    A   Asking the seed company   D   Looking at the seed VERY carefully
    B   Sequencing the parents   E   All of the above
    C   Growing several generations and seeing no change

10 _____ An F_2 monohybrid Mendelian cross consists of which of the following?
    A   Two heterozygous parents   D   A 1:2:1 ratio of the gentoypes
    B   A single trait with two phenotypes   E   All of the above
    C   A 3:1 ratio of the dominant/recessive phenotype

11 _____ What is a simpler way to perform a Mendelian test cross?
    A   Cross your unknowns with a recessive control   C Self the unknown, see results
    B   Perform a genetic test on the unknown   D All of the above

12 _____ Which of the following is NOT seen in autosomal dominant diseases?
    A   Two unaffected parents   D   Heterozygote individuals are affected
    B   The same frequency between sexes   E   All of the above are seen
    C   2 unaffected parents have no affected children

13 _____ This inheritance pattern can be identified by numerical-based traits
    A   Mitochondrial   D   Quantitative/multifactorial
    B   Sex-linked   E   None of the above
    C   Lethal

14 _____ Which of the following is NOT seen in X-linked recessive diseases?
    A   Two unaffected parents   D   Heterozygote individuals are affected
    B   The same frequency between sexes   E   All of the above are seen
    C   2 Affected parents have 100% affected children

15 _____ This inheritance pattern only affects one sex in Humans
    A   Mitochondrial   D   Autosomal recessive
    B   X-linked dominant   E   Autosomal dominant
    C   Y-linked

16 _____ The most common X-linked disorder in Humans
    A   Dwarfism   D   Swyer syndrome
    B   Color-blindness   E   Down Syndrome
    C   Hemophilia

17 _____ This inheritance pattern is only passed on from one sex in Humans
    A   Mitochondrial   D   Autosomal recessive
    B   X-linked dominant   E   Autosomal dominant
    C   X-linked recessive

18 _____ This technique introduces Cisgenic modifications into a genome (Indicate all that apply)
    A   Backcross   D   Gene Gun
    B   Agrobacterium   E   Polymerase chain Reaction
    C   Lentiviruses

19 _____ This technique introduces Cisgenic modifications into a genome (Indicate all that apply)
    A   Backcross   D   Gene Gun
    B   Agrobacterium   E   All of the above
    C   Lentiviruses

20 ____   This marker is primarily used to determine disease/carrier status
    A   SSR   D   Restriction fragment length polymorphism (RFLP)
    B   SNP   E   Microsatellite
    C   Classical

21 ____   This marker is primarily used to determine parental status
    A   SSN   D   Restriction fragment length polymorphism (RFLP)
    B   SNP   E   Microsatellite
    C   Classical

22 ____   A CODIS fingerprint value of "15" means:
    A   There is a "15" chance of a match   D   There are 15 alleles
    B   There are 15 repeats in BOTH alleles   E   None of the above
    C   There are 15 individuals who match

23 ____   A CODIS fingerprint value of "15/18" means:
    A   There is a "15" chance of a match   D   There are 15 alleles
    B   There are 15 repeats in BOTH alleles   E   None of the above
    C   There are 15 and 18 individuals who match

24 ____   A CODIS fingerprint value of "245/259" means:
    A   There is a "245" chance of a match
    B   There are alleles with 245 and 259 repeats respectively
    C   There are 245 and 259 base pairs in the two alleles
    D   There are 245 alleles
    E   None of the above

25 ____   Indicates that a trait is controlled by two or more genes
    A   Polygenic   D   Hybrid Vigor
    B   Quasi-trait locations   E   All of the above
    C   Multi-trait phenotype

26 ____   The trait controlled by Gene A is only seen when gene B has a dominant allele. This is an example of:
    A   Hemizygous Gene A   D   Hypostasis of Gene A under Gene B
    B   Epistasis of Gene A over Gene B   E   None of the above
    C   Hypostasis of Gene B under Gene A

27 ____   Pigment of a flower is controlled by a single gene. there are three phenotypes: Black (BB), Grey (Bb) and white (bb). This is an example of:
    A   Heterosis   D   Complete dominance
    B   Hemizygous   E   Over-Dominance
    C   Incomplete dominance

28 ____   You are within 1 standard deviation of the average height for your sex. What percentage of the population is taller than you?
    A   16%   D   95%
    B   34%   E   99%
    C   68%

29 ____   "Luck of the draw" inheritance is based on:
    A   Random organelle segregation   D   Finding a rich spouse
    B   Gambling during pregnancy   E   Genomic allele sorting
    C   Nuclear Chromosome segregation

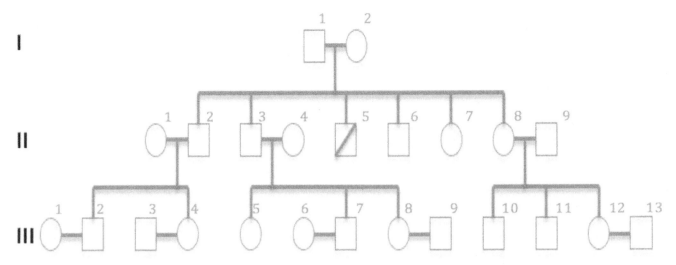

Starting genotypes: I-1 150/160; II-4 130/170; II-9 120/130; III-2 130/160; III-4 160/160; III-5 150/170; III-7 120/130; III-12 120/170

Answer questions 30-33 using the following simple sequence repeat genotypes, complete (as far as you can) the pedigree above – You will have to derive several genotypes.

30 ____ Which of these is a possible genotype for II-2?
   A   140/120   D   160/120
   B   120/120   E   unable to determine
   C   130/120

31 ____ Which of these is a possible genotype for III-8?
   A   140/120   D   160/120
   B   120/120   E   unable to determine
   C   130/120

32 ____ Which of these is a possible genotype for II-5?
   A   160/120   D   140/120
   B   120/120   E   unable to determine
   C   130/120

33 ____ Which of these is a possible genotype for II-1?
   A   160/120   D   150/120
   B   130/160   E   All are possible
   C   130/120

34 ____ Mendel crossed homozygous parents with Yellow (YY) and green (yy) seed to make yellow F_1 seed. These F_1 seed were then selfed. What is the percentage of seed in the F_2 generation that will be yellow?
   A   0%   D   75%
   B   25%   E   100%
   C   50%

35 ____ Suppression of a maternal or paternal copy of a gene has been linked to:
   A   Differentially Methylated Regions (DMRs)
   B   Selective Methylation
   C   Genomic Imprinting
   D   Suppression of gene expression based on methylation
   E   All of the above

36 ____ Mendel crossed homozygous parents with Yellow (YY) and green (yy) seed to make yellow F_1 seed. These F_1 seed were then selfed. What is the percentage of seed in the F_1 generation that were homozygous yellow?

A   0%   D   75%
B   25%   E   100%
C   50%

37 ____ You cross homozygous pea plants with Tall (TT) and short (tt) height to make F_1 plants that are *taller than either of the parents*. These F_1 plants were then selfed. What is the percentage of progeny in the F_2 generation that are taller than either parent?

A   0%   D   75%
B   25%   E   100%
C   50%

38 ____ A couple is concerned that a rare autosomal recessive disease occurs in both of their families. Tests confirm that they are both carriers for a SNP that causes this disease, in which the wild-type 'A' is mutated to a 'G'. What is the chance any child will be a carrier?

A   0%   D   75%
B   25%   E   100%
C   50%

39 ____ A couple is concerned that a rare x-linked recessive disease occurs in the mothers family. Tests confirm that they are both carriers for a SNP that causes this disease. If they have a child, what is the chance they will *not* be a carrier or affected?

A   0%   D   75%
B   25%   E   100%
C   50%

40 ____ In a cross between parent 1 AaBbCc x Parent 2 AaBbCc, what is the chance in fractions of having the genotype AABbCC?

A   1/2   D   1/16
B   1/4   E   1/32
C   1/8

41 ____ This molecular marker type is commonly used for criminal investigations

A   SNP   D   Isozyme
B   SSR   E   Classical
C   RFLP

42 ____ You wish to determine the genetic composition of an animal that is showing a dominant trait (B/?). You cross with another animal that shows the recessive trait (b/b). What is the genotype of the unknown if HALF of the 10 progeny show the dominant trait?

A   B/B   D   Either A or B
B   B/b   E   None of the above
C   b/b

93

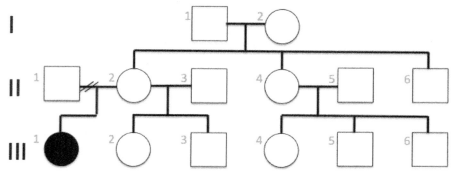

43 Who is the proband in the above autosomal recessive pedigree?

44 What is the relationship between II-1, II-2 and II-3 in the above autosomal recessive pedigree?

45 Who MUST be a carrier in the above autosomal recessive pedigree?

Marker	Child 1	Child 2	Child 3	Product	Father 1	Father 2	Father 3
TPOX	216/220	227/237	220/237	216-264	220/220	216	227/260
D3S1358	99/147	99/112	147	99-147	130/147	130/147	112/134
FGA	158/300	246/300	300	158-314	158/300	158/314	246
D5S818	129/165	136/154	129/136	129-177	129/177	129/177	130/154
CSF1PO	316/320	312/320	320	287-331	316/320	287/320	294/312
D7S820	194/216	234/234	194/200	194-234	200/216	200	234
D8S1179	157/209	160/182	185/209	157-209	157/185	157/185	182/203
TH01	171/184	184	171/184	171-215	171	171/215	184/206
VWA	160	136/160	122/130	122-182	130/160	130	136/163
D16S539	156/280	129/177	129/349	129-177	280/349	129/349	163/177
D18S51	284/322	309/320	284/322	262-349	322	262/300	309
D21S11	164/272	194/242	180/242	154-272	180/272	180	194/235

Allele sizes reported in ascending order and do not indicate parental source. Product is the size range for the marker. Assume that the mother is the same for all three children.

46   Based on the paternity data above, who is the father for child 1?

47   Based on the paternity data above, who is the father for child 2?

48   Based on the identified fathers, what is the mothers genotype for TPOX?

49   Based on the identified fathers, what is the mothers genotype for VWA?

50   If you have three siblings from two parents, how could you prove shared paternity (In other words, could you be sure that all three had the same father) without testing the parents?

Population Genetics Exam

1 ____ No Mutation is a Hardy-Weinberg assumption (True/False)

2 ____ An insertion of 3 bp is more damaging in a gene than a deletion of 1 bp (True/False)

3 ____ An insertion of 1 bp is more damaging in a gene than a deletion of 3 bp (True/False)

4 ____ An insertion of 1 bp is more damaging in an exon than a deletion of 23 bp in an intron (True/False)

5 ____ Chromosome duplications are caused by non-disjunction (True/False)

6 ____ An autosomal chromosome deletion is more lethal than an autosomal addition (True/False)

7 ____ A limited number of mutations in a gene indicates that it is likely to be central to the organisms survival (True/False)

8 ____ The wild-type allele is the most common allele in a population (True/False)

9 ____ A frameshift mutation removes a single codon and allows the polypeptide to continue growing (True/False)

10 ____ A population of 100 people has 4 homozygous recessive affected individuals. This means there are 32 homozygous unaffected individuals in the population (True/False)

11 ____ PGD + IVF enable us to introduce non-carriers/unaffected children into our population (True/False)

12 ____ Macro-evolution has led to many new species (True/False)

13 ____ The world was populated only after we domesticated plants and animals (True/False)

14 ____ The portion of a phenotype that is caused by the environment is considered to be...
   A   Heritable   D   Central
   B   Transmittable   E   None of the above
   C   Migrational

15 ____ Once a spontaneous dominant mutation has occurred in the progeny of a cross, it will become phenotypically evident at what time?
   A   When the affected individual mates with a sibling
   B   When the affected individual mates with a cousin
   C   When the affected individual mates with another affected individual
   D   In the progeny that inherited the dominant mutation
   E   All of the above

16 ____ A germ cell mutation that results in under-expression of many genes
   A   Chromosomal duplication   D   Sex Chromosome accumulation
   B   Autosomal dominant reversion   E   Chromosome deletion
   C   Sex Chromosome Y-linked inversion

17 ____ A somatic-cell mutation has which of the following characteristics?
A   All offspring are affected
B   One parent must be a carrier
C   Both parents must be carriers
D   The condition cannot be transmitted to progeny
E   The condition must be transmitted to male progeny

18 ____ Disease A is autosomal recessive. A total of 16% of the study population of 100 people are affected. How many carriers are in the study population?
A   12   D   48
B   24   E   60
C   36

19 ____ Identical twins were separated at birth. 34 years later, they found each other and were surprised that both of them were 5' 6" tall. This is an example of:
A   Environmental influence   D   Mutation selection
B   Natural selection   E   Reproductive success
C   Heritability

20 ____ A long-term study of Finches has been conducted on an island. After 192 generations, their progeny have separated into two distinct populations that are no longer able to create successful offspring between them and survive on different food sources. Why?
A   Macro-evolution   D   Micro-evolution
B   Natural selection   E   Environmental influence
C   Heritability

21 ____ Which of the following sequences would result from the annotation c.72dupTA[4]? THINK CAREFULLY!
A   5' …AUCACUAUAUAUACAGAUA..3'
B   5' …ATCACTATACAGATA..3'
C   3' …ATCACTATACAGATA..5'
D   5' …ATCACTAATAATAACAGATA..3'
E   5' …ATCACTAUATTACAGAUA..3'

22 ____ What is true of the "serial founder" effect?
A   All people of African descent are founders
B   All people from Europe are from a completely different gene pool
C   At each new founding event, genetic polymorphism is reduced in the new population
D   At each new founding event, genetic polymorphism is increased in the new population
E   None of the above are true

23 ____ You are a carrier for a disease. You wish to remove any possibility that the disease allele will be transmitted to the next generation. Which of these can accomplish this (multiple answers possible)?
A   PCR   D   Mating with an unaffected individual
B   IVF+PGD   E   Not having any children
C   IVF only

24 ____ Indicate all that are Hardy-Weinberg Assumptions (be careful!)
A   No Neutral Selection   D   No migration
B   Random meeting   E   All of the above
C   No mitigation

25 ____ Which of the following mutations is the most problematic for an organism?
A   2 bp deletion in an intron   D   6 bp deletion in an intron
B   3 bp deletion in an exon   E   Unable to determine
C   1 bp insertion in an exon

26 ____ Which of the following mutations is the most problematic for gene A (3,846 amino acids long)?
A   2 bp deletion in an intron   D   6 bp deletion in an intron
B   2 bp deletion in the 236th exon   E   Unable to determine
C   1 bp insertion in the 3834th exon

27 ____ Chromosome duplications are caused by:
A   Non-disjunction   D   Orthologous Mutations
B   Faulty Polymerase Chain Reaction   E   Paralogous Mutations
C   Mom-disjunction

28 ____ Region A of a gene has significantly less mutations than region B of the same gene. What could cause this?
A   Region A conserved due to necessary function   D   Region B is an intron
B   The region is GC-rich   E   Unable to determine
C   The region is AT-rich

29 ____ Allele A represents 60% of alleles in Human population 1, while allele B represents 54% in population 2. What can be said of this?
A   Both Alleles A and B are Wild-types   D   B is the disease allele
B   Allele A is the only Wild-type   E   All of the above
C   A is the dominant allele

30 ____ A population of 1000 people has 40 individuals who are affected by an autosomal recessive disease. How many are heterozygous unaffected?
A   32   D   640
B   256   E   810
C   320

31 ____ A population of 20 people has 5 individuals who are affected by an autosomal recessive disease. How many are homozygous unaffected?
A   5   D   20
B   10   E   Unable to determine
C   15

32 ____ Two healthy parents have nine healthy children, but their tenth child exhibits severe mental and physical issues. What is the most likely cause?
A   Chromosomal Inversion   D   Chromosome 21 non-disjunction
B   Autosomal Recessive disease   E   None of the above
C   Autosomal Dominant disease

33   Two related, healthy parents have two healthy children, but their third child exhibits severe mental and physical issues. What is the most likely cause?

         A   Chromosomal Inversion   D   Chromosome 21 non-disjunction
         B   Autosomal Recessive disease   E   None of the above
         C   Autosomal Dominant disease

34   Two unhealthy parents with similar symptoms have two unhealthy children with similar symptoms and one child that exhibits far more severe symptoms. What is the most likely cause?

         A   Chromosomal Inversion   D   Chromosome 21 non-disjunction
         B   Autosomal Recessive disease   E   None of the above
         C   Autosomal Dominant disease

35   Once a spontaneous X-linked mutation has occurred in the male progeny of a cross, it will become phenotypically evident at what time?

         A   The effects will be immediately apparent
         B   When the affected individual mates with a cousin
         C   When the affected individual mates with another affected individual
         D   In the progeny that inherited the dominant mutation
         E   All of the above

36   A mutation that cannot be transmitted to progeny

         A   Haploid cell mutation
         B   Germ cell mutation
         C   Somatic cell mutation
         D   X-chromosome mutation
         E   All mutations must be transmitted to progeny

37   A condition that is not transmitted to progeny

         A   Skin cancer
         B   Mosaicism
         C   Somatic cell mutation
         D   Patau syndrome
         E   None of the above can be transmitted

38   A germ cell mutation that results in *mostly* normal expression of several genes, but may affect fertility

         A   Chromosomal duplication   D   Sex Chromosome accumulation
         B   Autosomal dominant reversion   E   Chromosome deletion
         C   Chromosome inversion

39   Which of the following sequences would result from the annotation c.72dupCAG[4]? THINK CAREFULLY!

         A   5' ...AUCACUAUAUAUACAGAUA..3'
         B   5' ...ATCACTATACAGATA..3'
         C   3' ...ATCACTATACAGATA..5'
         D   5' ...ATCACTAATAATAACAGATA..3'
         E   3' ...ATCAGTCGTCGTCGTCAUA..3'

40 _____ At each new event, genetic polymorphism is reduced in *two* populations.
A   Natural selection events
B   Bottleneck events
C   Random mating events
D   Serial founding events
E   None of the above are true

41 _____ At each new event, genetic polymorphism is reduced in *only one* population.
A   Migration events
B   Bottleneck events
C   Random mating events
D   Serial founding events
E   None of the above are true

42 _____ You are affected by an autosomal recessive disease. You wish to remove any possibility that the disease allele will be transmitted to the next generation. Which of these can accomplish this (multiple answers possible)?
A   PCR   D   Mating with an unaffected individual
B   IVF+PGD   E   Not having any children
C   IVF only

43 _____ You are female and affected by an X-linked recessive disease. You wish to remove any possibility that the disease allele will be transmitted to the next generation. Which of these can accomplish this?
A   PCR   D   Mating with an unaffected individual
B   IVF+PGD   E   Not having any children
C   IVF only

44 _____ The polypeptide for gene A is 1200 peptides long in brain tissue and 900 exons long in bone tissue. This is an example of:
A   Smart mRNA   D   Alternative splicing
B   Tissue engineering   E   All of the above
C   Intron reorganization

45 _____ The transcript for gene A is expressed equally in brain tissue and in bone tissue. This is a likely example of:
A   A housekeeping gene   D   Alternative splicing
B   Exon shuffling   E   All of the above
C   A specific transcription factor

46 Disease A is autosomal recessive. A total of 16% of the study population of 100 people are affected. How many homozygous unaffected people are in the study population?

47 Disease A is autosomal recessive. A total of 91% of the study population of 100 people are unaffected. How many affected people are in the study population?

Use the following abstract to answer questions 48-50

PLoS Biol 5(5): e105.

A Dominant, Recombination-Defective Allele of Dmc1 Causing Male-Specific Sterility

Laura A. Bannister, Roberto J. Pezza, Janet R. Donaldson, Dirk G. de Rooij, Kerry J. Schimenti, R. Daniel Camerini-Otero, John C. Schimenti

DMC1 is a meiosis-specific homolog of bacterial RecA and eukaryotic RAD51 that can catalyze homologous DNA strand invasion and D-loop formation in vitro. DMC1-deficient mice and yeast are sterile due to defective meiotic recombination and chromosome synapsis. The authors identified a male dominant sterile allele of Dmc1, Mei11, encoding a missense mutation in the L2 DNA binding domain that abolishes strand invasion activity. Meiosis in male heterozygotes arrests in pachynema, characterized by incomplete chromosome synapsis and no crossing-over. Young heterozygous females have normal litter sizes despite having a decreased oocyte pool, a high incidence of meiosis I abnormalities, and susceptibility to premature ovarian failure. Dmc1, Mei11 exposes a sex difference in recombination in that a significant portion of female oocytes can compensate for DMC1 deficiency to undergo crossing-over and complete gametogenesis. Importantly, these data demonstrate that dominant alleles of meiosis genes can arise and propagate in populations, causing infertility and other reproductive consequences due to meiotic prophase I defects.

48   The defective Dmc1 allele is located on an autosome, yet acts disproportionately against male vs female fertility. Describe the effect that this would have on the approximate 1:1 Male:Female ratio in a population.

49   Describe a natural selection benefit to reduced meiosis that might explain propagation of the dominant defective allele.

50   Design an experiment that would test whether a mouse population with defective Dmc1 alleles actually does produce equivalent progeny to a wild-type population of the same initial makeup.

Central Dogma Exam KEY

1	F	coding DNA and template DNA have wrong direction (5' - 3')
2	F	
3	F	
4	F	
5	F	
6	T	
7	F	
8	T	
9	F	
10	F	
11	T	
12	F	
13	A	Only mitosis is associated with DNA polymerase; meiosis II does not replicate DNA; Ribosomal polymerase reaction is a foil.
14	B	The DNA template is used to make an RNA strand by RNA polymerase. microRNA is a functional RNA molecule, so there is no need to translate it
15	D	RNAse is a substance that destroys RNA
16	C	RNA polymerase is involved in the transcription of DNA into RNA
17	B&D	The PCR reaction uses heat to separate the two DNA strands, then DNA polymerase, primers and $MgCl_2$ are used to incorporate the nucleotides
18	D	Thermal cycler is a generic term for a PCR machine
19	D	A missing charged tRNA would stop the extesnion of a polypeptide chain
20	B	Turner syndrome is the only monosomic condition that results in a living Human
21	C	A 0.0 is a 0% chance of being a random match
22	C	A/T content and G/C content are exactly related to each other; G/C content more common measure of strand
23	B	In mitosis, the two resulting cells are equal diploid cells
24	C	Cysitc fibrosis is a specific, practical problem
25	D	
26	E	
27	B	Introns are removed from mRNA before mRNA is exported from the nucleus
28	D	There are always one fewer introns than exons
29	D	Only the removal of DNA from the heat-killed mixture led to living mice with no type IIIS bacteria.
30	A	
31	A	Only mRNA will be translated; rRNA and tRNA are functional molecules once they are transcribed
32	A	Although typically stated as G/C content, the A/T content also can predict the melting temperature Tm of a strand of DNA (the higher the A/T content, the lower the temperature required)
33	A	RNA polymerase is used for transcription of DNA into RNA
34	C	
35	B	
36	B	
37	A	
38	B	
39	A	ITS stands for internally transcribed spacer - although transcribed, the spacer must be sequenced to be of use in identification
40	D	This is about 1 in 1 million random chance (4^{10}) vs (20^3) or 1 in 8,000 for C
41	E	At first, this seems tough - just remember that for every five base pairs of DNA, you add three zeros; Thus at 20 base pairs, the chance of a random match is 000, 000, 000, 000 or 1,000,000,000,000 or 1 in one trillion.
42		3' - AGCAGCA - 5'
43		3' - ACGTTAG - 5'
44		5' - UUGCAUC - 3'
45		5' - CGAUACC - 3'
46		3' - AAGCGTA - 5'
47		rRNA, tRNA, microRNA, siRNA, mRNA, RISC, amino acids, polypeptides, etc.
48		Prokaryotes have a single origin of replication acting on a circular genome; Eukaryotes have multiple origins of replication acting on multiple, linear chromosomes

49	This is basic math with 4 to the sixth power; 4; 16; 64; 256; 1024; 4096; The odds are 1 in 4096 or 1/4096.
50	This is basic math with 20 to the fourth power; 20; 400; 8,000; 160,000; The odds are 1 in 160,000 or 1/160,000.

Transmission Genetics Exam KEY

1	E	Anticipation is indicated when a disease is presented earlier in each generation of a family
2	E	Heterosis is the condition where an offspring has a trait greater than either parent.
3	E	All of the F1 seed will be smooth - the smooth trait is dominant (note the capital "S")
4	E	All of the wrinkled seed are homozygous recessive
5	B	
6	C	The ratio gets closer to 3:1 as more data is taken
7	E	Band size represents the base pairs between two points in DNA; This is a phenotype
8	A	Our future is doomed if you picked plug-in….
9	C	
10	E	
11	D	A test cross is easily done by several methods that are less tedious than crossing two individuals
12	A	The are no unaffected individuals in dominant diseases
13	D	
14	B	Not "D"; female heterozygotes are carriers
15	C	
16	D	The most common disorder in Humans is color-blindness
17	A	
18	A, B, D	
19	E	All of these can introduce Cis (the same) genes into an organism
20	B	
21	E	SSN is not a marker type
22	B	
23	E	"15/18" means that the tested alleles have 15 repeats in one and 18 repeats in the other
24	C	
25	A	
26	D	
27	C	
28	A	1 standard deviation is 68% of the population. This leaves 32% remaining; half of these are taller, while half are shorter.
29	A	organelles are randomly segregated during mitosis into each daughter cell, meaning that each subsequent cell line is based on the organelles received during the previous mitosis events.
30-33		*Given genotypes: I-1 150/160; II-4 130/170; II-9 120/130; III-2 130/160; III-4 160/160; III-5 150/170; III-7 120/130; III-12 120/170; Derived Genotypes II-3 120/150, II-8 170, II-2 160/- II-1 130/160, I-2 120/170*
30	D	
31	C	
32	A	
33	B	
34	D	
35	E	
36	A	
37	C	All of the Tt plants are taller - this is a hybrid vigor/heterosis question
38	C	
39	C	Half of the daughters and half of the sons will not inherit the allele from their mother.
40	E	¼ x ½ x ¼ = 1/32
41	B	
42	B	
43		III-1; The proband is the person who brings the family under study and since tIII-1 is the only one showing symptoms of the disease, the would be the proband
44		II-1 is II-2s first husband and is relevant due to their child; II-3 is II-2s second husband, who is likewise relevant due to their two children
45		II-1 and II-2 MUST be carriers
46-47		*Identify the father by using a highlighter or colored pencil; the father is the only one who could have provided one of the alleles for every marker in the daughter.*
46		Alleles unique to **father 1** in child 1 are D7S820 216, VWA160, etc…
47		Alleles unique to **father 3** in child 2 are TPOX 227, D3S1358 112, etc…
48		216/237
49		122/160
50		Between the three children there are six alleles at each molecular marker locus, but only four alleles between the parents. If there are five unique alleles at any locus, there must be a second father. In the example below the five parental alleles for D3S1358 indicate a second father. It gets even easier with more than three children - there is still a four allele limit….

example:

Marker	Child 1	Child 2	Child 3	Parental alleles
TPOX	216/220	227/237	220/237	216, 220 227, 237
D3S1358	99/147	99/112	106/134	99, 147, 112, 106, 134

Population Genetics Exam KEY

1	T	
2	F	
3	T	
4	T	
5	T	
6	T	
7	F	
8	T	
9	F	
10	F	
11	T	
12	T	
13	F	
14	E	Environmental factors are not inherited
15	D	The progeny inherited a dominant mutation - it is immediately evident
16	E	
17	D	Somatic cells are not part of gamete production and new mutations cannot be transmitted to the next generation
18	D	start with square root of affected; $q = .4$, $p = .6$; $p^2+2pq + q^2$; $.6^2 + 2(.6)(.4) + .4^2$ $= 36$ unaffected homozygous + 48 heterozygous carriers + 16 affected
19	C	
20	A	
21	A	The sequence in A is mRNA (note the U's); a TATATA repeat would result in a UAUAUAUA sequence in
22	D	Each new event reduces the genetic polymorphism from the source population
23	B,E	
24	D	
25	C;	a 1 bp deletion causes a frameshift in a gene encoding region
26	B;	Frameshift will lead to very early termination
27	A	
28	A	
29	A	Wild types are the most prevalent in a specific population
30	C	divide the numbers given by ten to make the calculation easier....100 people, 4 affected; $q=0.2$, $p=0.8$.
31	A	.......20 people, 5 affected; $q=.5$; $p = 0.5$; (0.5 x 0.5 = 25% are affected, 50% heterozygous and 25%
32	D	Nine healthy children as carriers represents .25 to the ninth power or ¼ x ¼ x ¼ nine times or ~1/250.000 chance of happening with two carrier parents .
33	B	Relatedness of the parents means the most likely explanation is a shared autosomal recessive carrier condition
34	C	An autosomal dominant disease would explain this inheritance. The more severe symptom child is likely homozygous for the disease allele.
35	A	Males cannot be carriers of X-linked diseases; Progeny with the de-novo (new) mutation will have the disease
36	C	
37	E	
38	C	
39	E	complementary sequence to mutation
40	D	Only serial founding events cause reduction of polymorphism in the initial population and the group migrating from the initial population. (bottleneck affects only one population)
41	B	Bottleneck events occur to a single population and reduce their diversity
42	E	Autosomal recessive means that you have two diesease alleles - all children will be at least carriers.
43	E	Affected Females must pass on the allele to all children (E)
44	D	
45	A	
46	36	Start with square root of affected; $q = .4$ thus $p = .6$; $p^2+2pq + q^2$; $.6^2 + 2(.6)(.4) + .4^2 = 36$ homozygous unaffected + 48 heterozygous carriers + 16 affected
47	9	Start with square root of affected; $q = .3$ thus $p = .7$; $p^2+2pq + q^2$; $.7^2 + 2(.7)(.3) + .3^2 =$ 49 homozygous unaffected + 42 heterozygous carriers + 9 homozygous affected

There are many possible answers - the following is literally my opinion and should NOT be used as the sole grading source.

48 Although male fertility would be reduced, no change in the male:female ratio would occur - the number of males able to have children would be reduced.

49 Since there is apparantly little to no effect on litter sizes, this is a tough one. The difficulty in answering this question lies in the fact that as part of the litter, a carrier female would have 50% affected male offspring, essentially unable to sire the next generation. Perhaps an increased female mating drive might compensate.

50 The hypothesis is that a Dmc1 defective allele mouse population will produce the same number of progeny after "x" generations (you could use time as well). Providing consistent habitats and resources to both populations, you would allow the two populations to develop for the necessary generations/time, then you would count the number of progeny in each group. Perhaps creating data such as pedigree trees and Dmc1 allele status from each mouse. If the same number of individuals were in each group at the end of the study, you might change your hypothesis to a behavioural study, attempting to discover if a social cue was responsible.

Printed in Great Britain
by Amazon

81234471R00061